The Fox in the Chicken Coop

by Ric Bowser

God Bless You

Ric Brown

Copyright © 2007, by Ric Bowser

ISBN: 978-0-9802386-0-0

Library of Congress Control Number: 2007943116

Throughout the book the name 'satan' and related names are not capitalized even though this may violate grammatical rules.

Please note that unless specifically identified, the illustrations in this book are composite stories of actual clients. The names and details, however, are altered to maintain confidentiality.

Printed in the United States of America

FCM Pub.
www.familycounselingministries.com

Dedication

To Valee

Table of Contents

Genesis 3:1

Now the serpent [the original Fox In the Chicken Coop] was more crafty than any beast of the field, which the Lord God had made. And he said to the woman, "Has God said, 'You shall not eat of any tree of the garden'?"

Genesis 3:17

Then to Adam He said, "because you have listened to the voice of your wife, and have eaten from the tree about which I have commanded you saying, 'You shall not eat from it'; Cursed is the ground because of you; In toil you shall eat of it all the days of your life."

Genesis 3:24

So He drove the man out; and at the east of the Garden of Eden He stationed the cherubim and the flaming sword, which turned every direction, to guard the way to the tree of life.

Matthew 27:50-51

And Jesus [the perfect sacrifice] cried out again [from the cross] in a loud voice, and yielded up His spirit. And behold, the veil of the temple was torn in two from top to bottom, and the earth shook; and the rocks were split.

II Corinthians 5:17-18

Therefore if any man is in Christ, he is a new creature; the old things passed away; behold, new things have come. Now all these things are from God, who reconciled us to Himself through Christ, and gave us the ministry of reconciliation.

Introduction

She was perhaps twelve or thirteen when I first saw her, scared and withdrawn, with that look of innocence and helplessness that became so familiar to me. It was my second week on the job as a child welfare investigator for the county, and it was my first sex abuse investigation. I am guessing that most of us ex-child abuse investigators remember the first one. Without a doubt, were it not for her, I wouldn't be sitting here, in front of this computer, talking to you, for it was one of those defining moments in life that, for me, set my course for the next fifteen years.

Even if I could remember her name, of course I wouldn't tell you; neither would I bore you with the administrative details associated with a sex abuse investigation, except the one detail that played such a large role: this was my first involvement with law enforcement. I was instructed to call the sheriff, because I might have a *felony case* to investigate. Felony. That meant that if we actually proved a case against the offender/perpetrator, the result would be that he/she would spend some time in the state penal system. It all seemed so much like one of those detective shows I had watched on TV. When the deputy sheriff suggested we try a new investigative technique, I thought and hoped that he knew more about this than I did.

As it turns out, he didn't. Evidently he'd been to one of those continuing-education seminars officers are required to attend where they suggested a technique of having the victim make a phone call to the offender, while investigators listened in and tape-recorded the conversation. I know what you're thinking because it was *my* first thought: "Is that legal?" The answer is yes, evidently. You'll remember, this was my second week on the job, and I had only been briefly introduced to the complex legalities associated with my work.

After spending some time with the victim and gaining her confidence (evidently I have a gift for gaining peoples' confidence) she was willing to go along with our scheme. I mention this gift only because, for some reason, young and old alike wanted to tell me their life stories after what I thought was a fairly short period of time. These stories were not the ones about the grocery store or the softball game, but the ones with the intimate details which usually ended with, "I've never told that to anyone in my whole life."

We expected the going might get a little tough for a young, adolescent girl talking on the phone to the man who, as it turns out, was her natural father. He had sexually molested her, betraying all that is human and decent in a father, for the past six or seven years. (Excuse me if I get somewhat passionate here, for I have to tell you that for the next four years and over one hundred and twenty sex abuse cases, I never, never got used to the stories.) So we wrote a script for her to follow to make sure we obtained the incriminating information we needed. She sat there at my desk with the receiver in her hand, a makeshift *doodad* attached, whose other end was plugged into a hand-held tape recorder, while I called the number. A woman answered the phone, prompting a brief conversation which was followed by a request to talk to him. I do remember the admiration I felt for this young lady as I began to realize what was happening.

One moment I was sitting there with only a slight bit of apprehension born out of ignorance, playing detective with a deputy sheriff, when her voice began to change and become child-like. He was taking control of the conversation, instructing the girl who was becoming a little child to never tell those things to anyone. I am hard pressed to describe the look on her face. It was, and yet it wasn't, terror. Add in two parts shame and self-blame and still that wouldn't begin to describe what I was witnessing. I tried to make eye contact to reassure her, but she wasn't there and I am not sure who was. I had become part of a human drama for which I was grossly unprepared. How do you get your mind around the now obvious fact that there are people in this world who abuse the innocent entrusted to their care? The little girl who trusted me that day, pleading with her eyes saying, "Help me", didn't know I didn't have a clue how.

The next day I got a call from the deputy saying that, because we had used some cheap, dime-store recording equipment, the tape (which would have contained incriminating evidence due to the heroics of my little trooper) was too scratchy and therefore unusable. Some profanity followed about the department's budget and that was it. No case. Sorry. Literally, I was sick to my stomach and livid with rage at the same time. At that moment, I made a decision: never again. I knew I had much to learn about the darkness of the human soul, the callousness of the system, and the destruction of innocence. What I learned is what I am going to tell you in the pages that follow.

I tried to stay in contact with her. She said she didn't blame me, but beyond that I felt pretty helpless, especially when called upon to try to talk her out of the suicide attempts. The last I saw her, she was in her late teens and had had a baby and maybe a husband. She seemed OK, but I couldn't tell you for sure that she was.

Some years later (after I had left Children's Services and had taken on the task and responsibility of counseling with troubled children, adolescents, and their families) some common themes began to emerge. If one were to encounter someone like the young lady in the previous story at her moment of suicidal crisis, she would seem to the observer a troubled product of bad choices and capricious circumstances. But I knew her story. I knew the relationship she had to her caretakers and the messages they sent and she received. I also knew that her story was not all that uncommon except, perhaps, in the extremes of abuse and neglect. Yet, as I reflected on the world in which we live and the relational problems and issues we all encounter, I realized that all of us have our stories. We all find ourselves bewildered by the abuse and neglect of those who have power and control over us. We struggle to find our own way to survive only to discover that our survival styles are *causing* more problems than they solve.

This book is about you and me. It is about why we think and feel the way we do. In the pages that follow, we will identify four organizing principles as borders and boundaries to life's puzzle. This will help us to understand how the "mess of puzzle pieces" dumped on our tables are really supposed to look. We will obtain some answers to the questions: "Who is responsible for the circumstances in which we find ourselves? And why is responsibility so important?" We will explore ways of making changes and getting healing for our wounds that will actually bring us to where we really want to be in our most important relationships of life. These "high stakes" relationships include God, parents, and spouses.

There is a myriad of other relationships as well that we inevitably navigate in life from the boss at work to the clerk at the grocery store.

The word picture I use to help us understand the first and most important relational principle comes straight from the barnyard. It is simple and yet profound: when there is a fox in the chicken coop, the chickens *act crazy.*

It all began in the beginning when, as the Bible says, "Now the serpent was more crafty . . . (Gen. 3:1)." Evil was found in the garden of paradise and nothing has really been okay ever since.

A Parable

As farmer J strode into the barnyard that day, there was something in the air. It was heavy and oppressive, tasting almost metallic, as one labored to breathe. All of his senses went on alert as he, both consciously and unconsciously, pondered whether to fight or run from the unseen peril.

Slowly he made his way toward the chicken shed. Out they came screeching and squawking, half flying, half running, scrambling in all directions. There was blood and feathers everywhere. Farmer J didn't need to stop any of the chickens to ask them why they were behaving so crazily. He knew there was a fox in the chicken shed.

This had happened before. Back in '79, a fox had crept into the shed under the cover of darkness. Sometimes foxes crept in at night; sometimes they strode in boldly in broad daylight. Havoc and destruction had been wreaked in the chicken shed before any of the chickens even knew what had slithered into their midst.

It took considerable stealth and outright bravery and self-sacrifice on the part of farmer J to catch and put to death that sly old fox. But the damage had already been done. The chickens had been literally frightened out of their wits.

It was especially injurious to the young ones. Some of the old roosters had tried to explain that they had seen other foxes wreak their havoc on the shed, but always in the end, farmer J would deal out justice with the old, but effective, twelve gauge. Years passed before some of the hens could get back to laying eggs that weren't already fried, poached, or scrambled.

For years after, farmer J was at his wit's end with some of the hens and a couple roosters who seemed to lose all interest in food, fellowship and fertilization. From time to time, he would find one of the chickens hidden in the rafters, emaciated from lack of food with a glazed look in its eyes.

"We have medication for that," the vet replied to farmer J's queries about his chickens. "That's well and good," the farmer replied, "but what I am most worried about are the mean ones." Evidently some of the chickens had taken to terrorizing the shed after the last visitation from the fox. Farmer J couldn't understand why some of the otherwise pleasant and agreeable chickens had become so downright mean.

Farmer J was shocked one day to find crude little images of the fox molded from barnyard mud and stashed in dark corners of the shed. When he asked some of the older chickens what it meant, they told him that they didn't know for sure but that sometimes, at the turn of the day and the week, they would hear strange rhythmic clucking.

This concerned the old farmer deeply. "Perhaps we should call a meeting to talk about it," he suggested to the old rooster everyone acknowledged as the lord of the shed.

"That may not be such a good idea," the old rooster responded. "There is a lot of suspicion and mistrust of you right now. Why at times even my position and authority is questioned. Frankly, I sometimes fear for my safety. I can't blame the young ones though. Some of the old ones treat them very badly. There are those who even abandon the young in their charge altogether."

"We have decided to let some of the chickens try to talk to the ones having problems," the old rooster continued. "As a matter of fact, that's all some of them do." The old rooster obviously wasn't happy with the state of affairs in the shed, but the farmer could see he was doing the best he could.

There was a time before the fox came when chickens could expect to live their lives in peace and harmony under the benevolent protection of farmer J. Roosters would assume their position of leadership in the shed. Hens and chicks alike knew that both the farmer and the roosters would always act in their best interest to care for and protect them. There was harmony and unity of purpose, each chicken doing its job of assuming responsibility with love and devotion to the entire shed and especially to farmer J.

But, the fox of '79 had changed all that. Although the farmer knew he had blown that fox to smithereens, he always knew that some day there would be others. There was no way he could completely protect his chickens. He had in mind to teach them self-protection, but with their mistrust and, in some cases, down right self-pride (for you see some of the chickens thought they could handle the fox themselves or, at least, make a deal with him if they had to), it was difficult to communicate with the shed. This made the farmer very, very sad.

Fourteen years had passed since the fox of '79. In some ways things had gotten back to normal. Nests were built and eggs were laid. From outside the shed, it was hard to tell anything had ever gone wrong. But farmer J knew better. He had seen those now-mature chickens that were mere chicks in '79 grow up to be out-and-out strange. The chickens that had been given the responsibility to just talk to the others even had names for the strangeness. Pretty soon they forgot that it was the fox of '79 that started this whole state of affairs and began to tell the other chickens that some chickens were just plain born strange.

But here it was '93 and another fox had found his way to farmer J's chicken shed. With his twelve gauge in hand, he moved cautiously toward the old shed expecting to find yet another sleek, beady-eyed, marauding predator terrorizing the shed. What he found caused him to stop dead in his tracks, his jaw agape, dumbfounded in disbelief. Sure enough it was a fox, but his fur was matted and worn with age; his snarl menacing, but lacking in terror. It was the teeth though that bewildered the farmer. Over half were missing and many of the rest looked brittle or were broken. Not a speck of blood was on the old plunderer of chicken sheds; not one feather on his ancient fur to betray his previous activity.

The old fox was surrounded by a number of the older chickens. It was almost as if they were protecting the intruder. Farmer J was confused and badly shaken as he stepped back outside the shed to put his thoughts together and try to comprehend what he'd just seen. What sickened him to the core was the blood, not on the fox, but on the chickens themselves, dripping from their beaks and spattered on their necks and wings. And there were those crudely shaped mud likenesses of the fox himself lying on the floor in broad daylight.

As he stood there in total disbelief, the old rooster approached him from behind the hog pen. "You look like I feel," said the venerable old lord of the shed. The farmer slowly shook his head from side to side, able to mouth only two words, "What? . . . . Why?"

The old rooster motioned for the farmer to follow him behind the hog pen as he began to explain the events in the chicken shed over the past two weeks. "He just walked right into the shed as if he'd been invited." The old rooster began what was to be a long and mystifying story of power, intrigue, blood and betrayal.

"Why didn't you come to me sooner, " farmer J implored the old rooster somewhat angrily, but mostly brokenheartedly.

"Many times in the beginning I looked for an opportunity to talk to you," replied the beleaguered old rooster, "but, at first, I felt I could deal with that broken-down old fox. It wasn't until much later that his power became evident. There were others who thought they could handle things on their own, and yet other voices who pleaded for us to forewarn farmer J."

And then in a voice that evidenced the bitter irony that the old rooster felt, he told how the fox had been invited; how some of the chickens, particularly the angry one (though by now they had many labels) had had clandestine meetings with the fox to make deals to establish their own positions of power in the shed. Then the old rooster literally shivered as he spoke. "Not one drop of blood was shed until today," he sighed in exhaustion. "He did it all with a look."

Farmer J had heard enough. He was overwhelmed with sadness at the destruction of all he intended for his chickens, yet filled with righteous indignation and the knowledge that, whether they knew it or not, all the chickens must be rescued from the malicious deceit of the fox.

The old fox knew the farmer would be back. "He actually cares for these empty-headed, foolish fowls," he mused to himself. Surrounded by his duped cohorts, the old fox languidly lifted his head to peer at the figure of the foolhardy old farmer in the doorway. He had spent days stoking the fires of these imbecilic birds, filling their small brains with lies and hatred of the farmer.

The others he manipulated with threats and foreboding or silenced them with their own culpability for misdeeds long past. The young ones were especially ripe, and the easiest were those who had given up possession of their wills entirely and spent their days whining their way through life.

The scene before the farmer was a bizarre and sickening combination of blood and feathers, wounded chickens, and the strutting cocky cohort of brainwashed fowl. As he leveled his shotgun, he realized it would not be easy to shoot the intruder and leave the chickens unharmed. Moving cautiously toward the fox, he was confused to see that the fox not only didn't move, he hardly seemed to take notice of the farmer's presence. (Everyone knows, of course, that farmers have power over foxes, which is why foxes always steer clear of farmers with 12 gauges.)

The sly old fox had planned on this confusion in the mind of the farmer. With only the slightest twitching of his head, he signaled the traitorous attack on farmer J. Crazed chickens flew at him from all directions. But farmer J had anticipated the treachery. Bloodied and betrayed for the briefest of moments, farmer J wondered why he had even built the chicken shed. His second thoughts lasted only a moment however and, taking full responsibility for the shed and all the chickens, the old farmer blew yet another conniving and shrewd old fox to smithereens.

Many months passed before the farmer could talk again to the old rooster. "I don't know if they'll ever learn," the old bird observed. "Looking back, I realize in the end we were all deceived. A fox is a fox after all."

CHAPTER ONE

Authority/Dependency

The basic principle on which I operate is actually very simple:

When there is a fox in the chicken coop, the chickens act crazy.

Just what crazy looks like or feels like, well, that is where things become very complex. As a matter of fact, for the past 100 years, the science of psychology has been quantifying and codifying the inner workings of the human mind and have published their findings in what is called the *Diagnostic and Statistics Manual.* They have a term for everything, anything. For the sake of brevity, however, you'll have to excuse my use of the vernacular term, *crazy.*

The reason the chickens act crazy is that they don't feel safe. Believe me when I tell you that safety is the name of the game for us in the human race. Safety has a number of synonyms (one being, control) but, perhaps, the most accurate of them all is survival. The instinct to survive is built into us so deeply that many of our survival mechanisms, or styles as I call them, operate at levels completely beyond our awareness.

There is a story I remember my dad telling about a ten-year-old boy who, for his entire life, had never spoken a word. One morning as the family sat at the breakfast table (this being a number of years ago when families sat at breakfast tables) the child, quite out of the blue, exclaimed, "My oatmeal is lumpy." After retrieving dropped spoons and jaws, the family turned their attention to the child, not quite knowing how to respond. Finally the father said, "Why son, you can talk." The stunned silence now interrupted, the mother asked the question everyone was thinking. "Son,' she exclaimed, "Why, if you can talk, haven't you said a word for all these ten years?" To this the child, quite matter of factly, responded, "Up until now, the service has been fine."

While I suspect my father's story is fictitious, it serves to raise an issue of deep significance. What if, as a child, the service is not fine? This is a simple question with profound ramifications, reaching I suspect to the core of human existence.

Oh, I know what you're thinking: crazy chickens and mute ten-year-olds, the core of human existence? Sounds like a bit of a stretch. Well, hang on and give me a minute to explain. You see it has to do with the age-old question, "Why are things the way they are?" I believe that those crazy chickens and the mute ten-year-olds have something very profound to say. It is a concept that I call Authority/Dependency. I suspect that most, if not all, of the issues of life are born out of that relationship.

Ready or Not, Life Has Issues

You've heard it said, or maybe even said it yourself, "You know that so and so, well, he has *issues."* When he acts or reacts, he seems a little strange, edgy or overly sensitive, or maybe out and out weird. Like I said, we have codified all this strangeness and assigned medical terms such as obsessive-compulsive disorder, paranoia, passive aggressive personality or, the all-pervasive, depression. Many of these conditions have specific medications that have been developed to help ease the emotional pain or discomfort.

As you will see in the pages that follow, most (if not all) of the issues of life are a result of the interaction, or perhaps a better description would be the quality of relationship, between the person in authority and the individual in a dependent state. This relationship between authority and dependency is the defining concept in an understanding of life's issues. These issues of life come to us like the jumbled mess of a jigsaw puzzle dumped on our tables with no box cover to show us how it is supposed to look. The concept of authority/dependency will become for us the top border of our puzzle as we begin the process of making sense of life's issues and relationships.

Dependency

Let's begin by taking some time to define and describe just what I mean by Authority and Dependency. I'll start with dependency since that is our position in the first relational experience we encounter at birth. We are born into this life totally dependent. We don't necessarily remember being born (at least, not in a movie-like succession of events.) The reason for this is that we have not yet acquired language, which becomes the basis of encoding the event memories of our lives in our brain. And yet, we do come into this world with the capacity to interact with it emotionally. Furthermore, emotions have a memory. Whoever may have been in the room at the time of your birth probably witnessed an upset, crying, little bundle that (at that moment) was not particularly happy to be in this world.

Total dependency means just that. Our survival, both physically and emotionally, is totally dependent on someone else that most of us call "mom." There are certain circumstances, however, where a mom isn't present. Unless there is a caretaker to replace her, those of us born into such a situation are in trouble because we are so totally vulnerable to the harsh realities of life.

The essential characteristics of dependency are helplessness, vulnerability and naiveté. We are helpless in the sense that we cannot provide for our own physical survival and only minimally for our own emotional survival. We are, of course, then vulnerable to those or that which has power and control over us, naïve in every sense of the word, knowing nothing of the realities of this world (harsh or otherwise) that we have entered. If we have a caretaker, especially one who loves us, who has planned for us, and has awaited our arrival with joy and expectancy, in effect, we may be helpless, vulnerable and naïve, but we are not hopeless, or trapped, or already developing *issues.*

Authority

In order to be dependent, one has to be dependent on something or (more importantly) on someone. The core characteristics of authority are power and control. As you will see in chapter four, the concept of control is at the core of life's issues. I would go so far as to say that it is, in fact, all about control. If we don't have at least some sense of control of our physical and especially our emotional lives, we will find ourselves acting, in some way, like those crazy chickens.

Having authority means having the power to inflict pain or having the power to protect from pain those who are dependent. It means having the power to give or withhold the necessary physical and emotional nutrients of life. Authority also means having the

3

power to spoil or overindulge those dependent for their care. Acting in the best interest of children does not necessarily include giving them whatever they want. Authority can frustrate the plans, desires, or expectations of those in positions of dependency, sometimes for good reasons. There will be much more said about expectations later. In short, authority has the power to make us do anything we don't want to do.

The Power to Care

For the purpose of discussion, I will refer to all of the things authority has the power to do for us as *care*. Although care is a small, four-letter word, it is pregnant with meaning. Like a many-faceted diamond, care's multi-dimensions include the power to nurture, provide, protect, affirm and confirm, support, comfort, value, intercede, bless and release. I am also suggesting that when authority does not do all of the above that, in some way, our survival is threatened, both emotionally and physically.

Let's suppose for a moment that we are in the small, cluttered, cheaply furnished section eight (government subsidized) apartment of a young woman with two kids. One of the children is three months old with a dirty diaper and has just awakened, crying at two o'clock in the morning. What baby or mother hasn't had this experience? The problem is, however, that mom is doing crack in the next room with her boyfriend and is fairly oblivious to the cries of her child. The child's cries do get the attention of the boyfriend, however, who angrily yells at the mother, "Can't you shut that kid up?" Realizing that the mother is too far gone to be of any help to the child, the boyfriend takes it upon himself to *fix the problem* by slamming the bedroom door closed and yelling, "Shut up," at the top of his lungs. Unfortunately, now the child is both angry and frightened and stops crying only to begin screaming, readily provoking not just verbal, but physical abuse as well from the boyfriend. In the four years I spent as a child welfare investigator, I was called to investigate many such reports of verbal and physical abuse.

Let's switch the scene now to a similar-sized, modest apartment of a young couple that has also just had their second child. Dad has gone to bed early because he had to put in some overtime on the construction site where he has found work. Mom is also tired because their older child was up the night before with a flu bug. We find a similar scenario with a three-month-old child who wakes up with a dirty diaper. This mom awakens (for some reason that only mothers understand) just seconds before her child cries, anticipating that she would hear just that . . . the cry of her child. At the sound of her child, her milk lets down (she is nursing) and as she looks over at her husband, also slightly awake, she says, "I'll go." Upon entering the room, the first thing she checks is the baby's diaper, and sure enough, finds the problem. Although so common to thousands of years of mothering history, the next scene is crucial. Mom removes the dirty diaper, takes a warm wash cloth (hoping to be able to afford the package of disposable wipes some day) cleans the soiled area (one of the most sensitive areas on our bodies) dusts on some baby powder and puts on a clean diaper. Then the baby gets bundled up into a warm blanket, and mother and child sit down in the old, family-heirloom rocker where the child is nursed back to sleep.

These short moments of relationship between mother and child, or caretaker and infant are emotional, relational building blocks that will shape the child's view of the world and himself/herself for the rest of life. Crucial questions are being answered: Is this a safe place? Will I be cared for or do I need to care for myself? Can I trust that person who has the power of life and death over me or not? If the child decides that he can invest his trust, a bond is formed which becomes the basic building block of all relationships. This *ability* to trust is intertwined with the *bond* of trust and develops early with our first caretakers. When the relationship is one of abuse, a bond of sorts does develop, but it is what we call a traumatic bond. Traumatic bonds twist the soul and set in motion a lot of *crazy chicken* activities.

Life: A Series of Authority/Dependency Relationships

From the moment we are conceived, life becomes a progression of one Authority/Dependency relationship after another. There are certain of these A/D relationships that I call prototypical. In the most obvious example, parents (caretakers) and children have an A/D relationship. Parents have power and control, and children are vulnerable to that power and control. Other prototypical A/D relationships include teachers and students, bosses and employees, coaches and players, government and the people, priests and laity, and (interestingly enough) even the weather (and other natural forces that have power over us) and us. The most basic and vital A/D relationship is that relationship which exists between God, the Creator, and His creation. The history of the world is a record of this inter-relationship. There is also the authority of the culture or world in which we live. I call it the authority of public expectations. The culture has tremendous power to shape our thoughts, beliefs, and actions. Culture expects performance, conformance, competence and attractiveness. Armed with the power to shame, culture can label, stigmatize, ridicule and reject.

Will all of these authority figures always act in our best interest or will there be foxes in our chicken coops? We've all encountered foxes. And the foxes are not always so obvious either. Remember Little Red Riding Hood? That fox dressed up like grandma and was actually in grandma's bed. Family foxes are especially insidious because they betray all that we understand about what is right and good and how things *should* be.

When you were born into this world, you came as a *gift* (Psalm 127:3) to your parents. This gift was to be cherished and nurtured, loved and affirmed, and consequently, equipped to be the next generation to do the same for their children. In relation to this *positive* exercise of authority, none of us would have many issues. To some extent, however, most of us were abused, neglected, or over-indulged, sometimes all at the hands of the same authority. Of these woundings, it has been my experience that neglect seems to have the most profound, life-long effects, perhaps because neglect speaks to our deepest fear, the fear of abandonment. Hell itself has been described in various ways, including its being a place of eternal fire and damnation, or either way, a place of outer darkness. It is a place of eternal abandonment and separation from the Creator and sustainer of all that is seen and unseen.

We literally enter into a lifetime of relationships from the moment of conception. From the beginning, we journey through ages of dependency, maturing into first physical, then emotional adults. The psychologist, Mahler, suggests that our ability to negotiate the developmental phases of life is based on the quality of our Authority/Dependency relationships. Eysneck suggests that *psychoticism* (i.e.

craziness) has a higher frequency when we adopt negative attitudes and behaviors toward authority.

Positional/Relational Authority

At some point in our lives, we take on the position of authority. We become parents; some of us become bosses, teachers, coaches, policemen, priests, or adults with any number of positions of authority. I call this positional authority because it is different from assumed, or relational authority. Not all those in positional authority have relational authority. Relational authority is the result of having attained a high quality of relationship (one that has engendered a deep sense of trust) with those who are dependent on that authority. A bond of trust is formed and, in this place of dependency, there is a sense of well being. There, I am okay. The service may not be perfect or entirely up to my expectations, but I can handle the curve balls life throws at me because I am assured of care.

There is a scene in the movie, "Scent of a Woman," that in many ways describes the state of the culture in which we live as it regards care. The young, prep-school teen has won a scholarship to a prestigious, eastern school. He is from a broken home and estranged from his father. In a previous scene, he witnessed a prank by his wealthier, social peers and was put on notice that he would be called to testify against them. You can imagine his dilemma: rat on his classmates and become a social outcast, or refuse to testify and come under the wrath of the offended administrator. Enter a blind, ex-Army colonel whom the lad is engaged to accompany for a weekend in New York City. This retired colonel, of course, has his own issues, as many who have been in the military or politics have, and has plans to have one last fling in the Big Apple and then end his life with a bullet to the head. The movie is a fascinating exploration of authority and dependency, control and naiveté, and the profound effects one has on the other.

In the limo, as they ride to the City, the dilemma the young man is facing surfaces. Though reluctant to talk about it, he explains his situation. The colonel listens quietly and patiently for all the pertinent facts and then asks a simple, but profound and telling question. It is a question that reveals a deep understanding of authority and dependency, because generals (the good ones) understand these things. His question after hearing the boy's dilemma: "Where is your father?"

Fathers: The Buck Starts & Stops Here

In life, you see, we are meant to have fathers; not just biological fathers who have positional authority, but fathers who understand the sober responsibility they have to their children: to love, protect and cherish them; to teach them respect and self discipline; and to guide them into maturity, as one should who receives a sacred gift from God. For most of us, what authority really means is the power to rule over, the power to make the rules and have my own way. Who among us has not experienced the selfish, negative rule of those in authority? When this happens, we are then left to figure out how to survive, emotionally and physically, this abuse and neglect of true authority. These attempts at survival are called defense mechanisms. We all create our own unique defense styles. Perhaps these would be more accurately called survival styles.

While practically every Authority/Dependency system from the classroom to the work place, from the military to the church has a very structured handbook or manual, the most fundamental system that shapes us for the rest of our lives does not. There are no contracts or commitments to sign in order to become a parent. And yet, parenting is the most significant and influential pursuit in life.

Historically, the nuclear family has provided the model and training ground for the rest of life. The family, however, is in the process of redefining itself. Though some would suggest that biology or genetics is destiny, in essence, having the power to abuse, neglect, and overindulge is the power one in authority has to shape the human soul. Some (though very few) come to an understanding of the power to shape the human soul. Some also use that knowledge to enforce their own selfish wills. Unfortunately, too many fathers and mothers are unaware of the power they have to shape their children's souls. How many times have I heard the words, "She/He is eighteen now and old enough to make her/his own decision." And all too often, they turn over that decision making process before the child even reaches eighteen. Just because a child has a will doesn't mean he is ready to make good decisions for himself, let alone making the important ones like deciding on a value system, choosing friends, or even choosing who to marry. The choosing of a value system brings with it an authority system in, and of, itself. Children are placed under authority in A/D relationships for a very good reason. It takes time to grow up.

History, culture, and civilization (or the lack thereof) are the tales of the effects of that relationship on the soul. It would seem that with all the abuse and neglect, especially the atrocities of human history, the best answer would be to abolish all rule and authority. That way, with everyone equal and no one to rule over (I am using the term *rule over* as a synonym for the negative exercise of authority), we could live in something approaching utopia where there are no more tears and no more pain. But, as history suggests about the nature of man, all experiments in equality for everyone have failed. Someone, as it turns out, needs to be in control.

It's a Hierarchical World After All

The fact is that that is the way God made it. Created order is hierarchical with levels of designated authority. There is also an order of priority concerning those authority systems. God's first created Authority/Dependency institution was the family which has priority over all other A/D institutions. Satan, the enemy of all of God's created order, knows this and, from the beginning, has set out to destroy the family. This continues to be his strategy. His first encounter with humans was not a family meeting around the coffee table to suggest, with everyone present including the creator, the merit of talking over this *tree of the knowledge of good and evil thing.* You know the story. Satan has been dividing and conquering the family ever since.

Although the first husband, Adam, was placed in authority in the first family, it was never intended that he rule over his wife and children. Rather, he was to love and protect them as a cherished gift from God Himself. When the first family joined satan's rebellion, they were expelled from paradise. The effects of this have rippled down through history. If the strategy to divide and conquer the family worked then, why change? The family is as much under attack today as it was then. And still today, when the strategy is successful, the dependents are left vulnerable.

The family then was created to take precedence over all other created institutions. That includes work, school, government, and yes, even the church. Remember: the church, as we know it, has only

9

been a very recent player on the world scene and, in many ways, imitates its secular, non-believing, worldly counterparts.

In assuming authority and taking power and control, we believe in the old adage, "knowledge is power." We have to know and understand why things are the way they are. Co-existing within the human soul, we see the will (having the power to choose), along with the intellect and human emotions. As it turns out, these things called emotions are very powerful. It is to the power of these emotions that we now turn our attention.

CHAPTER TWO

Emotions Trump

The fact that we make decisions based upon how we *feel is* a core truth that those in positions of power and influence have found to be true and have capitalized upon time and again. Engaged in such diverse fields as advertising, politics and, of course, religion those individuals who would aspire to power and influence know how to use this cornerstone of human motivation. The left border of our puzzle of life's issues is something we all know instinctively to be true, though rarely admit: Emotions Trump.

If you are not familiar with my use of the term *trump* in this context, let me explain. "Trump" is a term used in many card games to identify a particular set of cards that, when played, override, outweigh and take precedence over the value of any other cards played.

That is the way it is with emotions. They are so powerful that, in the course of human events, they will almost always trump. I am tempted to say "always," but that may be too absolute. They will trump just about anything including logic, rational thought, values, beliefs and anything else we may believe we use as a basis on which to make decisions and respond to the events of our lives. It is not what is rational or logical or even our espoused beliefs that direct our actions. No, our actions and reactions are and will be governed by our feelings.

Emotional IQ

Some years ago, Daniel Goleman published his best selling book, *Emotional Intelligence.* It was subtitled: "Why it can matter more than IQ." In the book, Goleman painstakingly chronicles the scientific data on the power of emotions and how they rule our lives. I am also indebted to David Viscott for his introducing to the subject many years ago in his little book, *The Language of Feelings.* For, in fact, as it turns out, they have a logic and a language all their own. If we do not come to some understanding of that language and that logic, we do so to the detriment of our own sense of well-being and that of those with whom we are in relationship.

I have found, in my years of counseling and teaching, that it is this subject that is perhaps most misunderstood or just outright rejected. We just don't want to believe that we are ruled or governed by our emotions. Whether we're making the most important decisions of our lives, like choosing a spouse or a career, or dealing with much less significant decisions such as which toothpaste to use or what shoes to purchase, the fact of the matter is that it truly is all about *how we feel.*

How Do You Feel About That?

A common question I use in counseling is, "So, how do you feel about that?" I have to tell you that it is very unusual for the answer to include the description of a feeling. Usually the response is, "Well, I think . . . " and the person goes on to report a thought. Again I ask about feelings. Usually by the fourth or fifth inquiry about feelings, the person gets frustrated and comes to realize that it is difficult to report feelings, because they are not something people get in touch with right away. Sometimes I am told that the person is not the touchy, feely type. But whatever the resistance package looks like, it will inevitably surface.

How often have you heard it said that so and so is not in touch with her/his feelings? Well, why should he be? What is the big deal? When I want to check something out with a counselee, rather than saying, "What do you think?" I pose the question, "Does what I just said *feel* true?" Simply stated, it is what we *feel* is true that will change our thinking, not what we *think* is true that will change our feelings.

Evidently, those entrusted with the job of selling us anything in this life (from salesmen of shoes to candidates running for public office) understand very well that the decisions we make will not be based on some rational formula, but rather on just how we *feel* on any given day. Haven't all of us at one time or another said to ourselves after choosing a particular make and model of automobile, or after stepping out of the voting booth, "Well, I just had a good feeling about it or him?" The reality is that that is why we make the choices we do.

I suspect that you may not agree with all I've said. You may even be shaking your head at this moment. Perhaps I have somehow offended your sensibilities. And yet, when you think about it, being offended is a feeling.

Survival Feelings

There is a very simple reason for feelings having so much power to rule our minds. The reason is survival. Created in every one of us is the instinct to survive, which not only includes physical survival, but also (perhaps even more importantly), emotional survival.

The issues of life are what emotional survival is all about. Emotional discomfort left unresolved can lead to emotional pain. Our minds and our souls then respond in order to deal with this pain that has literally forced us to defend ourselves. Dealing with emotional pain is the same as dealing with physical pain, except that we don't take some physical action to avoid or minimize the pain. We take mental action to minimize or avoid the pain. If, however, the emotional pain becomes too overwhelming, there are some who choose to end their physical lives in order to be free of the emotional pain.

The trumping emotions to which I am referring are what I call the primary negative emotions of fear, anger and guilt. If we were referring to positive emotions, such as joy or happiness, that were dominating the system, well, then let them trump. We don't need defenses against positive emotions. If it were really possible to be happy and not worry on a regular basis, however, you wouldn't be reading this right now and I would have never felt compelled to write it.

In reality, we do experience pain in this life, both emotional and physical. It is imperative that we learn how to survive it. We call the actions that we take to do so, defense mechanisms. The continued use of particular defenses soon develops into a defense style. As I mentioned earlier, through the science of psychology man has explored, defined and codified these defenses and defense styles in the *Psychiatric Diagnostic and Statistics Manual.*

Survival Styles

But just what is a defense mechanism, or, as I call it, a survival mechanism? Probably the most common example would be denial. Something just hurts so much that we pretend or act as if it doesn't exist or didn't happen. You see this often upon someone's hearing tragic news. Perhaps a close loved one dies unexpectedly. What is our first response at hearing the news? We shake our head and say, "No, it can't be. I just talked to so-and-so yesterday." Something in our minds just won't permit us to think about or accept the unexpected loss, so we initially deny that it has even happened. While denial is one of the most basic and perhaps one of the most often used defenses, there is another thirty to forty common defenses we use on a regular basis.

I know what you're thinking. With all this pain and discomfort of life, and all these emotions trumping, it sounds as if every one of us is some sort of crazy. Not really. You'll remember that I suggested that "crazy" has more to do with functionality than insanity. Most people recover from and cope with the difficulties of life. That is why we have defenses to rely upon: they soften the blow and ease the discomforts of life, helping us to better cope. To some extent our personalities (what people perceive as who we are) are in fact the coping style we have developed throughout our lives.

Many people use their defense styles not only to help them function well, but to achieve levels of success they might not have otherwise reached. Take for example the young high school football player who, with his size, speed, and athletic ability, is regarded as a very promising college prospect. In the game of football, it is not just size and ability that sets you apart. Perhaps it has as much to do with attitude. Though the game requires that you have the ability to take punishment, it also requires that you have the ability to dish it out. As it turns out, the aforementioned athlete had both the physical ability and the attitude to "dish it out".

What if, however, there is more to the story? What if (one Friday night, just before a home game at the stadium) an assistant coach goes back to the empty locker room to retrieve a clipboard and hears an unusual noise in the shower room? Upon checking, he finds that promising young athlete in full uniform taking a razor blade, cutting himself, and using the pain and sight of his own blood to work himself into a rage. This, in fact, had been easy for him to do because the young man had much unresolved rage to draw upon. Following his ritual, he would take his rage/attitude out onto the playing field, using it to help facilitate his success in the game. Now, suppose that the issues that were driving this behavior could somehow be resolved? Do you suppose the young athlete would continue to be as successful? Maybe he would, but probably he would not.

You see, while we often use our defense styles to facilitate our success, a fine line exists between their normal use and the point which they become dysfunctional, as with our football player. Often in life, there comes a time when our defenses either don't work well enough to keep the pain or discomfort in check, or they finally stop working altogether. This is usually the time when a person will seek help from somewhere, something, or someone.

Survival Styles Can Become the Problem

It is not unusual, however, that the coping mechanism one employs becomes a problem in and of itself. In fact, most addictions to alcohol, sex, work, and food are attempts to ease or deal with the emotional pain.

Remember, now, the lessons taught in chapter one. Life is a series of A/D relationships. These relationships are played out in a series of transactional events that we experience through our emotions. While most of these events are social in nature, involving other human beings, we also encounter and interact with forces that aren't human, forces ranging from the weather to the animal kingdom to the spiritual forces that are at work in our world. We *feel* either in control of them or not. I will address at length these spiritual forces in a later chapter, but, just to set the stage, I believe as George Otis Jr. suggests in his book, *The Twilight Labyrinth,* that the spirit world is in fact the basement of reality.

Counselors often use lists of emotions to help people identify and get in touch with emotions, which, for one reason or another, they strongly defend against. Some of these lists are extensive, containing dozens of emotions and hundreds of nuances. For our purposes here, however, and for the sake of simplicity, the focus will be on what I call the three primary survival emotions of anger, fear, and guilt. A fourth category of sadness (relating to life's sorrows and grief) will also be mentioned. I call anger, fear, and guilt survival emotions because that is precisely their purpose—to facilitate our survival, and not just our emotional survival but our physical survival as well. Think about it with me for a second. If I had an unleashed, pit bull dog suddenly appear, growling and menacing as I jogged along a city street, quite quickly I would feel threatened and, consequently, afraid. The dog has the power to hurt me and seems out of control. Because of the connectedness between the threat and the fear, some refer to the fear as a secondary emotion. Without getting too technical, the fear is the primary emotion with which one needs to deal. As with all primary survival emotions, it is usually triggered by something else, in this case a threat.

Fear

I want to start our discussion of primary survival emotions with fear. Fear is perhaps the deepest, most primal, survival emotion of them all. Volumes are dedicated to an explanation of fear and all of fear's implications, nuances, and expressions. My intention here, however, is to give you a few informational hooks upon which to hang your understanding of emotions. It is also important to note why ignorance of their power leaves you unable to adequately identify them, unable to learn how to manage them, and unable to learn how to manage the emotions of others. We must recognize that not only do emotions trump, but also their application and use (as I will talk about in chapter four) help us to understand that it is also all about control.

Triggered by Threat

Most fears are triggered by a threat. In my jogging example, the threat was a dog. Threats though can be anything that potentially has the power to cause one pain, either physically or emotionally.

What in the World Is Homeostasis?

At this point in our discussion, I must say something about homeostasis. It is important because it helps us to understand why certain things happen in our brains causing us to think and feel the way we do. Somewhere in your home or apartment is an object called a thermostat that is hooked to a heating and cooling system, regulating the temperature in your home. One simply sets the dial at 72 degrees and the system does the rest. What you may or may not know, however, is that the temperature in your home is almost never 72 degrees. In fact, it probably varies from 70 to 74 degrees depending on how the system is set up. What actually happens is that when the temperature reaches 70 degrees, your heating system turns on. When it reaches 74 degrees, it shuts off until it falls back to 70 degrees, and then turns on again. The heating system in your home is actually maintaining what is called homeostasis, a comfort zone that is flexible, not constant (as is true of the rest of our universe which contains very few rigid constancies).

Our emotional moods, of course, are similar. They rise and fall with all the vicissitudes of life while maintaining an emotional, homeostatic comfort zone. If things become too painful, our defenses will kick in. The same is true at the other end of the continuum. If we become too emotionally high, something tells us to calm down. For most of us, that sense of well-being is somewhere in the middle.

This homeostatic process usually has a life of its own, that is, it goes on without our being aware of what is happening. Because emotions are so essential to our survival, they often don't have time to check with our sense of rational thought, or even our value and belief systems. Like the Apostle Paul said, "That which I want to do, I don't, and that which I don't want to do, I do." Goleman calls it the amygdala hijack. The amygdala is the part of our brain that sits at the top of our spinal column and is the primal source of emotional response. This part of our brain, by the way, is *not* very well connected to the parts that do our rational thinking, which is why emotions *will* trump.

Temporary States

Emotions were made to be temporary states. After an event triggers an emotion, certain things are supposed to happen to facilitate our survival. I call this the cycle of resolution. In the pit bull dog/fear example, we either confront and fight the threat or get the heck out of there. We call this the "fight or flight" response. A third response, when overpowered by fear, is to freeze. This is potentially a very dangerous reaction because it does not lead us to safety. The ultimate goal *is safety* and, when achieved, we experience the resolution of the emotion. Once safe, we literally don't need the emotion any longer.

What happens, however, if we can't get to a safe place? What happens if, in an A/D relationship in our dependent state, we are stuck or trapped in a physically or emotionally dangerous place that is truly painful? What if that place is the home in which we grew up or a schoolroom or the work place? What if there is a fox in our chicken coop? We have to survive and that is where our emotional defenses are intended to come to our aide. Also, if you remember, many (if not most) of those defenses operate outside of our level of awareness. This can all become quite complicated.

Pain & Place

At the risk of making it even more complicated, it is important to note that we associate pain with place. Each place has it sights, its sounds, and its smells. You probably don't consciously remember your first visit to the doctor: those white coats, institutional green walls, the smell of antiseptic and maybe even the smell of lunch on the doctor's clothes. At first, none of this mattered. Mom was probably there reassuring you that everything would be okay. It was not until the doctor started sticking things down your throat and poking around, making you feel uncomfortable, that you began to say to yourself, "I don't think I am going to like this place."

And then, there she was (in her white dress with that *thing* in her hand) ready to give you a shot. She said it wouldn't hurt much, but IT DID. Even though they gave you a sucker, it wasn't much comfort. It was then that you made the decision somewhere in the back of your mind, that in order to avoid any more pain, you would never go back there again. But, it really didn't matter. Any time you got sick, they took you there "for your own good." And, for some reason, just the smell of the place always made you sick.

Emotions get entangled with all the "stuff" that triggers them. Depending on how intense the events, they may never get untangled. The fact of the matter is that most of us don't take the time to be in touch with our emotions, let alone examine them. The truth of the matter is that if an emotion doesn't come to some resolution, it will linger indefinitely.

Emotions Know No Time

I remember years ago when my daughter, who was about five years old at the time, was with me one evening when I stopped by my office. On our way out, she ran ahead of me down the stair well. (She always had a streak of independence in her). Seconds later, I heard a blood-curdling scream that I knew was coming from my daughter. As I ran down the stairs, I found her cowering away from two very large, black dogs who were now also spooked and barking. They were both on a leash, and the owner was holding them back and apologizing for the encounter. I scooped up my daughter, trying to calm her down and to reassure her that she was now safe. From then on, she had an issue with large dogs. Just recently, she bought a puppy as a pet for her oldest child. Of course, it is one of those fluffy, little things that will grow no bigger than ten pounds. Because emotions do not just go away with time, they can last a lifetime if not resolved.

Anger

While fear's goal is to get us to safety, anger's goal is to level the playing field. Remember that survival emotions are triggered in A/D relational events. Anger's triggers are primarily hurt and frustration. Something or someone has the power to inflict pain or withhold something we desire. Because anger feels more powerful, it is not unusual for us to use anger in order to mask other less powerful feelings, such as fear or guilt or even sadness. Anger, for example, is actually one of the earlier stages of grief.

Suppose one day you are on your way to the fridge for a snack when, not really paying attention, you accidentally put your hand on a hot burner. "Someone "has left the stove on. A series of fairly predictable events are now set in motion, beginning with your quickly pulling your hand away and saying the first cuss word that comes to your mind. I know what you're thinking, "I don't use cuss words," and maybe you don't, but remember there is no one around and your hand really hurts.

Profanity: The Language of Anger

The reason you *may have* used profanity is that profanity is the language of anger. Someone who uses a lot of profanity probably has a substantial amount of unresolved anger. I've found that the professions employing the most profanity (in some cases, making it an art form) are the military and police-type organizations. I imagine that when you deal with homicidal elements in any society, you feel a need for some empowerment.

Anger: A Distancing Emotion

Note the connection of physical pain to anger and remember that anger is the emotional reaction to pain. Also notice that you moved your hand as far away from the source of pain as possible. That is because anger is a distancing emotion. When we are angry because of being hurt, we push people away so that, with the distance, we can feel some safety and control.

Ascribing Blame & Regaining Control

What happens next is interesting since we usually need to ascribe blame to someone or something. I know *blame* sounds like a bad word and, after cussing, why do we need to talk about blame anyway? In reality, blame has gotten a bad rap, because as with anger, it is essential to the process of resolution.

"Who left the stove on?" The answer to this question, as you will see, is essential to our well-being. If I was the one who left on the stove, essentially there is no problem. I can be angry with myself, perhaps *beat myself up* somewhat (if that's what I do) and then resolve to be more careful in the future. On the other hand, if my child left on the stove, there is no problem either. I can scold him and, with a few threats, assure myself relatively well that he won't do it again. In either case, my anger is resolved because I am back in a safe place and in control. If, however, whoever left on the stove is positioned above me in the A/D hierarchy, then I do have a problem because they have the power and control. Once I inform them of their neglect, how will they react? Will they care about my pain and act in my best interest, or will they abuse or neglect me, causing me more pain? So I take the risk and say, "Mom, the stove was on and I burned my hand." As soon as I say it, I know I shouldn't have, because her response is, "It's your own darned fault. If you would just pay more attention, those things wouldn't happen."

What if, however, I had a mother who said, "I am sorry you hurt yourself, sweetheart? Okay. Come here and let me look at it. Don't worry. I'll try to be more careful."

What happens to the unresolved anger with my fictional mother's first response? The anger does not just cease to exist, because emotions don't just resolve themselves. It is not unusual for the anger to come out sideways towards someone or something else, like a younger sibling or the family dog. Sometimes, our anger gets redirected toward ourselves. Anger needs a target, but if the object of our anger is someone in authority over us, then it may be that the only safe target for our anger is ourselves. The anger may get redirected into a defense mechanism such as a passive-aggressive stubbornness, or foot-dragging, or a sarcastic attitude, especially toward authority. How many of us took out our aggressions playing football or basketball, or fighting with our younger siblings or someone on the playground, or even ending up getting sick with some flu bug. I've always wondered if perhaps the reason we call it *catching a cold* is because our bodies are actually responding to experiencing a lack of warmth.

Anger Can Serve Our Purpose

Anger serves many purposes in our lives. Some of us become angry due to the chaos around us, in an attempt to create order. We become angry at the lack of intimacy, to create intimacy. We become angry at feeling trapped, in order to have the power to break free. We become angry to gain respect or just to feel empowered. Although it may seem backward, we sometimes get angry to avoid conflicts.

Be Angry and Sin Not

Anger is one of those emotions that, if we don't monitor it closely and engage our thinking/decision-making powers, can become very counter-productive. In the letter to the Ephesians 4:26, Jesus tells us to be angry but to not sin. Being angry is not the sin, but its expression can be. From the sin of self-hatred to hostility and revenge, anger is like driving a muscle car at high speed. It feels powerfully exhilarating but can get out of control in a heartbeat, not to mention all of the intricate emotional defenses we may use to deal with it, consciously and unconsciously.

While assessing blame is part of the process, it does not resolve our anger. The goal here is safety. That is why we put the distance between the source of our pain and ourselves. If the person with whom we are angry is someone with whom we *want* to be in relationship, or someone in authority with whom we have to be in relationship, the distance needs to be resolved. In the final analysis, only forgiveness in the true sense of the word resolves anger. Forgiveness that does not resolve anger excuses or minimizes the offense or even forces reconciliation. True forgiveness occurs when one truly ends up paying the price for another's offense and, by choice, absorbs the pain himself/herself.

Unresolved Anger

The opposite of this is the unresolved state of anger evidenced in hostility, the desire to hurt the person who hurt you, i.e. the desire to take revenge. When this desire reaches an extreme level of intensity, rage occurs: revenge is taken with no regard for whom gets hurt.

Guilt

While it is easy to see how fear and anger can be labeled survival emotions, where does guilt fit in? Simply stated, without guilt, we would cease to survive as a people. One of the most defining qualities of a socio/psychopath is that he/she can injure and/or kill others without any feelings of guilt or remorse. How long would the human race last if we lacked guilt? As with all emotions, guilt is not an "either/or" proposition. There are varying degrees of guilt depending upon the condition of the human soul and upon the situation.

While fear is triggered by a threat and resolved with safety, anger is triggered by hurt or frustration and resolved with safety and forgiveness. Guilt is triggered when we feel that we have offended someone or a set of accepted values. When I have offended/hurt someone, I feel badly, repentant and remorseful. I want to "make it up" to them in some way, paying the price for my offense, and receive their forgiveness, or absolution, for my offense.

When I have offended a set of values, such as civil laws or moral values, again I feel remorseful or repentant and am ready to pay for my offense and resolve my guilt. Guilt can penetrate to the core of authority/dependency relationships, for when I have offended, often I have caused another pain and have thus put myself in a position of authority with the power to do so.

Lacking guilt or remorse, as described by sociopathology, can also speak to the issues of pride, rebellion and competitiveness. The resolution of these issues looks more like humility than anything else.

Unresolved Guilt

The unresolved state of guilt usually looks and feels like shame. Not only did I do something wrong; now I believe that there is something wrong with me. This gets really tricky when those in authority use this as a tool to govern and shape behavior. How many times did you hear the phrase, "shame on you," when you were growing up? How did it feel? Do you still hear those words nagging somewhere in the back of your mind? Remember: feelings know no time and, if they are not resolved, have the power to trump at any given moment, for no apparent reason.

Without being too technical here, shame can also be defined as the fear of exposure. There is badness in me or perhaps I am just stupid, ignorant, clumsy, ugly or all of the above. My unworthiness and ineptitude are obvious to all and my shame is the scarlet letter I wear on my breast.

I think that she was perhaps twelve or thirteen when I first met her. I was working for the welfare department investigating complaints of neglect and abuse. One common complaint we received was what we referred to as a dirty home complaint. I know what you mothers are thinking. You didn't have a chance to rid things up for a couple of days and yesterday's dishes are still in the sink. Can someone report me for a dirty home?

The dirty homes I am referring to are far beyond your comprehension of normal clutter and neglect. This particular house was old and in a sad state of repair. Upon entering the front door, which only opened enough for me to squeeze in sideways, I was hit with that nauseating smell that became so familiar. Trash and clutter were piled literally to the ten-foot high ceiling and there were pets that treated indoors as if they were outdoors. Yes, this was the definition of a "dirty home."

She was very shy and reticent to talk, but we finally calmed her and gave her a sense of safety. It was then that she began to share her story. She lived with her mother who was chronically absent from her life. If she wasn't working, she was playing bingo six nights a week. Her father had died a couple of years before. It is her story prior to his death that I want to share with you.

From what I could gather, he was an alcoholic and a mean drunk at that. After work and a stint at the bar, he would come home, roaring drunk, and proceed to find and molest his daughter before collapsing into his nightly stupor. One of those evenings as he came through the door, the frightened little eleven-year-old ran to her room and hid under her bed to escape his abuse. She talked about hearing him stumble up the stairs roaring her name and threatening severe punishment.

He found her in her room, forced the door open against the clutter, and realizing she was under the bed, tried to grab her, but, lacking coordination, raged in frustration. At that moment she lifted a prayer to God for His intervention. "Please God, take me or take my father." At that moment in time, her father fell dead of a massive heart attack.

Imagine the confusion in her mind. Had she caused the death of her father? In the time since that event she had had no resolution from her sense of guilt. I told her that it was not her fault. I made sure that, not one time in all my talks with the hundreds of young victims I counseled, would I neglect to tell them, "This was not your fault." But, I wonder how many actually believed me. After all, what power did I have to affirm them? What authority did I have to establish their self worth? For only those who have established the "bond of trust" can actually change a belief.

False Guilt

She was experiencing what we call *false* guilt, which is the belief that big people don't make mistakes. Therefore, when bad things happen, it must be *my* fault. It may be false guilt, but it can be more real than the actual guilt we should feel at real offenses. The long-term belief system it engenders can dominate the emotions/emotional landscape for a lifetime and be transferred to generations of dependents who follow.

Absolution Resolution

Triggered by offenses, these feelings can only be resolved by absolution. At the core of absolution is forgiveness, true forgiveness . . . the self-sacrificing, the taking upon oneself and paying the price for the offense. It is much like a financial transaction where resources are transferred to another account to be returned at a later date. Offenses that invoke pain, which can be termed "abuse" or "neglect," literally become a spiritual transaction held in account in the spiritual world of ultimate reality. Literally speaking, when someone offends, hurts, or neglects you, they come into your debt. In other words, they owe you.

This transaction remains open until closed by the payment for the offense. We are instructed in the Lord's Prayer to ask for forgiveness of our sins/offenses as we forgive those who sin against or offend us. In our financial example, if we were to forgive a debt someone owes us, who in fact pays the debt? Obviously, we do. The same is true of these spiritual/relational transactions.

Paul tells us that satan is the accuser of the brethren. Just what is it for which we are being accused? If our sins have been forgiven and covered by the blood of Jesus (i.e. paid for) and there is no record of them kept, to what can satan allude as a basis of accusation? I am suggesting that these open transactions are the basis of his accusations. And, evidently he has the spiritual right to harass both parties. In the Old Testament, the repayment of debt was to be of equal value, an eye for an eye, a tooth for a tooth. Jesus said, "Forgive those who sin against you." It is at the moment of forgiveness that both parties are released from the debt because the debt has been paid.

Sadness

The last of the survival emotions is sadness, the feeling that we experience when we have lost something significant. While feeling sadness may not seem to facilitate our survival, if you have ever lost someone very significant in your life, you may feel at the time like you do not want to survive another day. Often the worst time is when we feel completely alone and there is no comfort to be found.

Sadness seems to respond only to time and comfort, comfort being the sense that we are not alone. I have found that when the loss is deep as in the loss of a cherished loved one, there are really no words to say. It is only my physical presence that can speak words of comfort to the soul. In these times of grief, one must understand that there is a process through which it takes time to walk. One model of that process has been presented by Kubler-Ross. In that model, the stages of grief include sadness and other survival emotions.

25

One does not just bounce back from severe loss, whether of a loved one, a job, a home or the devastation of a fire (these losses of everything are extremely traumatic), or loss of respect or position. These threats to our survival are reminders of our own mortality and require the actual engagement of the emotion to be resolved. Often it is the engagement of that emotion that we avoid, much like we do used car salesmen.

Compounding Survival Emotions

It is not uncommon that with a traumatic loss, other survival emotions will creep into the process. This complicates and delays the healing and resolution. One of the first things I try to determine when dealing with a client who has suffered a severe loss is whether there are other negative survival emotions connected to the loss. Is there any feeling that he/she is responsible for the loss, thus complicating the issues with his/her guilt?

Often their anger is at someone "leaving" them with this mess or not keeping their promise to care for them. Obviously, the mess of emotions experienced by the young girl previously mentioned will take years to sort out and resolve if the process is even attempted.

Chronic Sadness

The shades of loss in life are many—from the loss of a cherished loved one to the loss of a favorite pair of shoes. But, it is in each of these losses that our survival seems threatened. The state of unresolved sadness or chronic sadness is depression. When I encounter someone who is depressed, at some point in the conversation I ask the question, "What have you lost?" Usually the answer is that they have lost hope . . . hope that these unresolved emotional states will ever be resolved. It is impossible to count the number of depressed persons I have heard say, "Nothing ever changes."

Although it is time and comfort that facilitate the resolution of loss, when a person feels the burden of sadness lifted, it is usually because he has regained some sense of hope. It is here that those with an abiding faith in God and His promise of eternal life find hope. On the other hand, if this life (without God) is all there is, hope may be hard to come by.

Any of our survival emotions has the POWER to trump at any moment in time. Each A/D relationship has the power to trigger our issues from any previous A/D relationship. If any of the unresolved states linger, and of course they do, we find ourselves in funks that sometimes we can get a handle on, but often we cannot.

Just Get Over It

At this point, I want to say something about the "get over it" mentality. It sounds something like this: Why dwell on the past? Why blame my parents or some frustrated old-maid schoolteacher? Or, in even more extreme trauma caused by criminal activity, why can't we just deal with it or, better yet, get over it? Picture a battlefield, full of wounded soldiers with torn and shattered body parts. Into this scene comes the colonel himself, disheveled, shouting and exhorting the wounded to rise up and fight. Some of them may try or may even will themselves to rise to the battle. But their broken bodies prevent them from picking up arms or standing to move forward. No matter how strongly they will themselves to battle, they cannot.

Emotional wounds are deceptive. There is no blood or obvious deformity. The defense systems employed to deal with the wounds appear looking dysfunctional or even bizarre. Consequently, those attempting to deal with their wounds using these defense systems are rarely seen as wounded—only as sick, weird, or crazy. And, of course, the last thing one wants to communicate is that he or she is *crazy*. Sometimes in therapy, the most therapeutic thing I can say is, "You're not crazy."

I know what you're thinking: that I am suggesting that somehow, some way, we are all victims and that we should see ourselves in that way. And what about the ones in our society who actually *play* the victim, adopting a victim mentality? No, that is not what I am suggesting. The fact is that emotions trump because they are that powerful. If we really want to move on with some sense of resolution and control, these emotions must be dealt with and resolved. To deny or ignore their power is, in itself, a defense mechanism and, in fact, by default, emotions *are* trumping.

CHAPTER THREE

Two Shots In Life

As the couple sat in my office engaged in yet another verbal battle over the state of affairs in their shaky, twelve-year marriage, it was obvious that there was much more at stake than household chores, budgets, the kids, or even sex. In twenty years of listening to marital squabbles (and inasmuch as every couple says that the "biggest" problem they have in their marriage is communication, money, or intimacy) I can tell you that it really boils down to the fact that one or both do not sense that the other really cares for him/her and nurtures the relationship as expected. This is, in fact, why I call these squabbles, *Care Battles.*

We Are Born to Expect Care

The battles come from a deep sense of knowing in our souls that we only get two shots in life to receive the care and nurture we are born to expect. Yes, born to expect. Our understanding of life's expectations is the third border of life's puzzle. We are not conceived and do not develop as a blank slate or some fetal blob waiting to pass through the birth canal as a human being with all the related rights and privileges. Rather, some time during our development in our mother's womb, we embrace the understanding that the nutrients of life will be provided for us by our caretaker as we rest safely encased in this protective bubble. Then at birth, our worlds are rocked by our separation from the safety of the womb. We come into the world expecting that all the misunderstanding will be taken care of by the *big* people. We will be fed, kept safe, warm and dry. We will be held and talked to, cuddled and nurtured, both physically and emotionally.

First Shot

Our parents are our first shot at receiving the nurture and care we deserve in life. I say *deserve* because we are told that children are a "gift" from God (Psalm 127:3).

As babies, we get uncomfortable with dirty diapers, upset stomachs, too much noise or the many other harsh realities of life, we let out a cry, and the *big* people respond and make things okay. It is a pretty good system really: we cry; they respond; and all is well with our world. A bond of trust is formed between those nurturing us and ourselves. With this comes gratitude and humility on our part.

We don't really mind doing what we are told to do because we have come to believe it is in our own best interest to do so.

For many of us, however, the mother and child images of the turn-of-the-century Impressionist artist, Mary Cassatt, are far from reality. One difficult dynamic I have come to understand in my work as an investigator for children's services is that when a child is seriously abused or neglected over a period of time, often he/she eventually stops crying. Even at the tender stages of infancy, one comes to understand that his/her expectation of care will not be met, and he/she ceases to attempt to communicate his/her needs.

I was impressed with the reality of this truth one day as I sat in the doctor's office looking around for a magazine to read. I noticed a picture hanging on a bulletin board. (By the way, have you ever noticed that if someone had led you blindfolded into a doctor's office that you would know almost immediately the doctor's area of expertise by looking at the magazines? It is hard to find a *Car & Driver* or *Sports Illustrated* at your wife's gynecologist's office.) The picture that had captured my attention was of tiny, twin newborns, bundled up and lying on their tummies. One of the infants had reached out its little, spindly arm and laid it across her sibling's shoulder. It is one of the most moving photos I have ever seen. The photo was entitled, "Rescuing Hug." Evidently, the babies had been born prematurely and placed in separate incubators. They were not expected to live. A nurse, defying hospital rules, had placed them back together in the same incubator. When reunited with her sibling, the healthier of the two threw her arm around her sister, whereupon the smaller baby's heart rate stabilized and her temperature rose to normal.

We are born to expect that the service will be fine. But many find this to be (as an old, college buddy of mine used to say) "a rough ole world." Sometimes it can be a very rough place indeed.

Preverbal trauma is especially difficult to address, whether it is the trauma of abusive slaps, shakes, and shouts, or the trauma of neglect, where physical and/or emotional nutrients are withheld.

This trauma causes great pain and leaves deep wounds that require some form of emotional defense. Many people talk about the pain that they have felt all of their lives. If the pain originated at a time prior to when they began talking, it will seem to them that they were born this way.

We Expect Relational Connections

Our expectations of care go way beyond just the need for food and shelter. We are human and, consequently, we have an expectation of relational connections that *make* us human and separate us from the plant and animal world. We expect such relational amenities as love and kindness, care and protection, support and affirmation, warmth and (certainly not the least) meaningful touch. This is the way *things* "ought-to-be." We all know what the *ought-to-be's* of life are.

Ought-To-Be's

When things are not as they ought to be, our souls are profoundly affected. Some of us become angry and carry that anger into our A/D relationships. Much of our response actually depends on our genetic/emotional predisposition since, in fact, we inherit a major portion of our personalities. If our family's survival style is to become angry, there is a good chance we will also. Or if the family tends toward fear and anxiety, we will often end up there. All of this occurs before we can even talk, before we can put words to our feelings and thus encode the events of our lives in the thinking part of our brains. Consequently, we lack the ability to retrieve them later. Instead they become exclusively pain encoded in our emotional memory. *Talking* therapy is of little help against such pain, and chemicals merely anesthetize it. Truly only the Holy Spirit, who was present at our creation, can assist in identifying and healing the source of this pain.

The effects of abuse and neglect are often seen in infants who are given up for adoption. The little three, six, or twelve-month-old looks so helpless and in need of love and nurture. Lovingly, you pick up the child with the sole purpose of giving her/him the affection she/he so needs, only to have the child respond with a piercing scream, arch her/his back, and pull away from you. No matter how you may try, the child will not be comforted and begins to throw a fit. Contrast this experience with that of the child who has

31

formed a firm bond with his/her mother, who (when reluctantly handed to you) conforms to your body and coos. The neglected infant has already changed its expectation of care and has begun to build walls to gain some sense of safety in his/her little world. Not all infants given up for adoption develop a bonding or attachment disorder. Some are born (having stronger genetic fiber) with the strength to survive emotionally better than their peers.

The Parenting Failure of Overindulgence

Not all *parenting failures* are the result of abuse or neglect. Some parents are over-indulgent. Overindulgence can also damage the soul. Selfish pride lurks in the human soul and, if not checked by those in authority, can result in a self-centered, egotistic, narcissism that may cause untold destruction of lives and relationships. Sometimes one of the responsibilities of those in authority is to protect us from ourselves and from our own selfish pride. Parenting success involves walking a fine line of encouraging self-confidence while discouraging self-centeredness.

Unintentional Neglect

In addition, not all negative bonding issues are intentional. Some of us are born into this world with medical conditions that result in our needing intensive medical care. We may have to spend a considerable amount of our early lives in hospitals or separated from our caregivers because we need special medical attention. Sometimes our caregivers have medical conditions that take *them* away from *us*. Within my own family, we suffered the loss of a young mother of newborn twins when they were merely seven days old. Fortunately, the children received wonderful care from a surrogate for their first two years of life and later from a very dedicated stepmother who will raise them to adulthood.

Of course, not all of life's traumas occur in infancy. Many experience the harshness of life at other stages in the developmental process. The good news is that children have the unique ability to adapt and recover from trauma. What I have found is that in the stages of growth before puberty/adolescence, children can be shaped and molded like wet mortar with a trowel. Once puberty hits, however, things begin to change fairly rapidly. It is not that teenagers cannot be shaped and molded, but rather that the mortar begins to set and, instead of a trowel, one has to use a hammer and a chisel.

Growing Up Is Hard To Do

While I have spent some time addressing the extremes of unmet childhood expectations, I must say that, to some degree, most of us have our own unmet expectations of care. The issues of our own neglect or abuse do *not* go away as we grow up. In fact, they boldly resurface with each developmental crisis of life that we encounter. The first major occasion materializes at puberty, the time in our life when our bodies betray us and commence doing all sorts of strange things. Because we are already in a state of crisis, everything that has been nailed down emotionally starts coming loose. And, by the way, most of this transpires in places in our souls of which we are not even aware.

It was just a bottle of aspirin that got one of my clients into trouble. He was at the drug store alone (for whatever reason a thirteen-year-old would be there). Picking up a bottle of aspirin, he stuck it in his pocket, and walked out the door. His action did not go unnoticed by the store manager who, being fed up with kids who had been shoplifting in his store, decided to *make an example* of this one. The police were called, charges were filed, and a court date was set. Fortunately for this young man, the judge sensed that there was more to address below the surface of the incident and chose to do more than just teach a lesson.

Consequently, there they were (mom, dad, and son) sitting like three, plaster-cast imitations of a family at their first, court-mandated counseling session. I asked them to tell me why they were meeting with me. Both parents threw visual daggers at junior as if to say, "This is all your fault. You tell him." The story was quickly rehashed. I looked at the young teen and asked if he had had a headache that day. He said, "No." I took a wild guess and said, "You probably had the money in your pocket to pay for the aspirin. Is that right?" And he said, "Yes." I glanced at the parents long enough to see them roll their eyes. I decided to forge ahead and ask *the big one*, "So, why did you steal the aspirin?" And he responded, "I don't know."

There it was: the inevitable, *I don't know.* The parents were, by then, totally exasperated. The father voiced his frustration with, "You put us through all this and you don't know WHY?"

While the answer to "why" may have been obvious to me, it wasn't obvious to junior or his parents. There was, needless to say, something wrong within the family system, but everyone involved was far too emotionally *hijacked* to be able to see the forest for the trees.

The "something wrong" within the system was exactly why the young man had stolen the aspirin. The service was *not* fine. In this case, there was plenty of food, shelter, and clothing, and nothing (really) that would be described as abuse. The father angrily pointed this out by saying, "So, what do you mean you don't know?" The problem was the boy *really didn't know* and often we don't.

To the drug store merchant, junior was just a juvenile delinquent, lacking in moral fiber and deserving punishment. "Lock him up; it will teach him a lesson." I think the parents might have even agreed. The fact of the matter is that there are selfish, prideful, and even malevolent people in this world. The truth is that junior was just not one of them. We all have sinful natures. Who among us has not said, "There, but for the grace of God, go I"?

Emotional Neglect Has Profound Effects

I soon learned, in junior's case, that he had suffered profound emotional neglect. The parents allotted no time to spend with him, to take an interest in who he was or what he did. There was very little affirmation or meaningful touch. As it turned out, their past six weeks' involvement in the juvenile justice system was the most time they had ever spent together as a family. When (generation after generation) family systems accept abuse and neglect as a way of life (as "the way it has always been"), and parents say, "I dealt with it. Why can't you?", eventually the result is an appearance in juvenile court or worse.

Unmet Expectations of Care Become Longings As We Grow Up

When unmet, the expectations with which we were born turn into longings in adulthood. Longings are extremely powerful, emotional motivators that have great impact on us when choosing the person, our spouse, who will serve as our second shot in life. Once again our hope is to receive the care and nurture we were born to expect.

Longing is a sibling of loneliness and, at times, it is difficult to distinguish one from the other. How many times have you heard it said, or even said yourself, that one can feel lonely in a crowd of people? How often have couples reported that they have been married for years but, for some reason, still feel lonely? This often results in sighs of frustration from the other spouse and then the question, "What do you want?" This usually brings the response, "I know what I want, but I just can't put it into words. "

How Do We Put Our Deepest Longings Into Words?

By the time we reach our mate selection years (which is approximately late adolescence) we believe that we have a fairly good understanding of love.

We are naturally attracted to those who will receive our love and give theirs in return. Adolescence is a creation of our modern industrialized society. It is that span of time in life between our being physically capable of bringing children into this world and, later, our being emotionally and physically responsible enough to be parents. This discrepancy in timing is, in effect, why we teach our children to not have sex and babies until they have finished school, obtained a job and are emotionally ready to be responsible spouses and parents.

It is a good idea to have parents who are emotionally ready to be responsible adults. As we all know, this is often (if not usually) not the case. Dysfunction and irresponsibility breed dysfunction and irresponsibility. We have generations of unmet expectations and longings, as well as the emotional and often physical destruction that comes with it.

Second Shot

Although I have read conflicting data on the subject, it has been my experience that opposites attract. It is our unconscious desire to fill in the gaps of our emotional make-up. For example, the high-strung are attracted to the "laid back," the task-oriented to the relational, and so on. When one decides to marry one's opposite, however, there is a lifetime of emotional-relational hard work ahead. It seems the couple is forever trying to "get on the same page," which makes this second shot all the more difficult to achieve.

Looking For the Ideal Parents Often Ends In Co-Dependence

It is not unusual that, when selecting a spouse, we start by looking for the ideal parent we either never had or don't want to leave. Often, unknowingly, we enter into co-dependent relationships that, within a few years, turn into nightmares. I define co-dependence as my emotional beliefs connecting with your emotional beliefs in negative ways. Suppose you became a nice, sweet, pleasing-type because that was the only way to get along with your angry and petulant father. Suppose I am charming and engaging, and you like being with me despite my infrequent petulance of angry outbursts. Of course, your sweet, pleasing ways are viewed as a sure remedy for my ways once we are married. The problem is that they seldom remedy anything. It is not until a couple of kids later that you finally realize that God isn't going to change me despite all your prayers. It is not that God couldn't change me. He *could.* But, my free will is involved.

Resolution To Longing = Indulgence of Desire

At each developmental crisis in the marriage, including first child, job changes, mid-life and so on, the longings resurface. The longer they remain unresolved, the more powerful they become. Somewhere along the line comes the notion that the resolution to longings is the indulgence of desire. Indulging desires can look like anything from consuming comfort food to cocaine; engaging in pornography to an affair; being a workaholic to finding one's identity in one's children. All of this we justify to ourselves, knowing that if we don't take care of our own emotional needs, no one else will.

We, in fact, often marry someone who we believe will be successful in caring for and nurturing us. Our hope is, of course, that this time we will get it right. In many ways, we look for our ideal parent who will resolve our longings for care. Unfortunately, too often we find ourselves in co-dependent relationships that not only do not resolve the longings, but rather tear the scabs off the old pain.

In over fifteen years in the counselor's chair, refereeing and mediating marital squabbles, arguments and sometimes out-right war, it has been my experience that practically every fight boils down to one basic issue. It isn't money or sex or communication. It is one spouse trying to say to the other, "You don't care for and nurture me as I expected and now long for." Of course, the other spouse says the same, but adds that if only the *other* cared, then he/she could also care. An argument ensues over whom should go first—the classic *Care Battle*.

Depression = Loss of Hope

I am convinced that a large part of what we diagnose and treat as depression is the loss of hope that the expected care and nurture will ever come. If there is no God who really loves and cares for me, then I am of all creatures to be most pitied.

You Go First

There are those relationships where one or the other member has a stronger sense of how to meet the other's needs. This individual understands the ought-to-be's and goes about the hard work of making it happen. Usually the woman is the natural nurturer, although the man can be just as nurturing. Consequently, it is left to the natural nurturer to "go first." This is precisely, however, where the A/D relationship comes strongly into play. If the natural nurturer does not have positional authority, she finds herself in the worst of all places: in the middle between feeling the responsibility and having no authority, power, and/or control to "make it happen."

She or he, but usually she, wears herself out serving the needs of the spouse and family, eventually burning out. This burn-out may manifest in one of various ways including a nervous break down or shut down, depression or panic attacks. Emotional pain may convert to physical ailments. In such cases, however, it is difficult to know what came first: the emotional pain or the digestive disorder. Stomach or digestive disorders can be directly related to dependency/nurturing disorders. How many heart problems, lower back problems, joint problems, migraines and hormonal issues are connected to deep, unmet longings for care, nurture, and safety?

Often the spouse is not really to blame. He or she didn't really know that for which they were signing on. It often comes as a surprise to the husband (who has positional authority) when I tell him, "You have now taken on the responsibility of resolving your spouse's issues. You are now her second shot, and it is essential that you get it right." But, where is the manual for that? Marriage, like parenting, doesn't come with a manual. Yes, there are a wealth of marriage "how to" books, tape series, and seminars. Many of them are very helpful. If this core issue of care and nurture is not addressed, however, all attempts, even with the best of intentions, will miss the mark, leaving a nagging sense of longing and loneliness.

It is here, at this crucial point in the proceedings, that resolution becomes exceedingly difficult because these longings are needs that require *someone else* to fulfill them. Therefore, we find ourselves as a *dependent* in the relational equation. As dependents, we have developed various survival styles to cope with neglect that then kick in. We now become our own worst enemy. We continue to carry around all the old baggage, attempting to make relational lemonade from the lemons of unmet expectations, feeling helpless and hopeless, sick and depressed.

I Empower You To Fix Me

How often have you encountered someone with real pain who you really want to help? All of those who serve in the helping professions are sensitive to those in pain. Therefore, you try to help only to find that you get enmeshed in the other person's life, spending large chunks of your time in conversation in person or on the phone. It is almost as if you have become their second shot at getting the care and nurture they were born to expect. They literally place you in an authority position and empower you to fix them with your care. Have you then tried to set some appropriate boundaries, only to find that you receive their anger in response to your, seemingly, callous neglect?

Those who have not connected in their spirits with the ultimate authority (who created us for relationship with Him) are of all people most miserable. I am not talking about a relationship based on a set of doctrinal beliefs. Many of these doctrinal belief systems become yet another authority system that, in and of itself, is abusive or neglectful. Who hasn't attended or heard about toxic churches?

Theology = Survival Style

For many others, their beliefs in God are merely extensions of their own survival styles projected onto their God. Projection is a defense mechanism, taking our beliefs about life and (in slide projector fashion) projecting them onto someone else's screen. Suppose, for example, that I hate myself, which is an uncomfortable emotional state. To deal with this discomfort, I project that self-hatred onto you by saying, "You hate me, don't you?" This is, of course, not true. But it seems that no matter how sincere your attempts, you remain unable to convince me that you indeed do not hate me. Often God has the same problem with us.

What I Know = What I Have Experienced

God's intention, from the beginning, was to be in relationship with us, His creation, in an *experiential* way. Adam walked with God in the garden and, for him, that must have been quite an experience. Experiences in life are "experienced" or lived through our emotions. Oh, I know what you're thinking. Emotions and feelings are so subjective that we can't rely on them as a basis for knowing. The fact of the matter is, however, that we do not only rely on them, we base most of our relational decisions on them. While it is true that facts affect our relationships, it is our emotions that provide a genuine sense of connecting in this life. Remember, emotions trump.

Of all the people who have profoundly impacted my life (second after my own father) my father-in-law, whom I affectionately knew as Deno, continues in his legacy. Deno died two days after our first wedding anniversary. Consequently, none of my children ever knew him. Deno lives on in our hearts and minds and in the "bigger than life" stories we experienced with him. For you see, Deno really was bigger than life. It will always be a point of sadness in me that my children could never "experience" him.

One day while visiting my mother-in-law in her room full of memories, she showed me Deno's discharge papers from the Army. He had a purple heart from injuries sustained during World War II, from the loss of a finger and shrapnel wounds in his neck and leg. He also had two bronze stars. I don't ever recall Deno complaining or even talking about those wounds, except for one time. We were eating our lunch on a hot summer day, sitting in the kitchen of a house under construction. We were installing the rough plumbing and were glad for the opportunity to take a break. I don't know how we got on the subject, but I do remember asking him about the war.

He began to share about "Omaha Beach." He had been there. He spoke only briefly about swimming through and stepping over the bodies approaching the shore. The conversation seemed to end abruptly, and we went back to work. I remembered that conversation as I read his Army record, standing in that room with my mother-in-law. There on the discharge papers was just one, seemingly inconsequential reference to a place, "Normandy."

Many months later, my son asked if I would like to go to a "guy" movie with him. Seeing as how I love movies and time with my son, it was a "no brainer." I'd seen some of the previews, but was in no way prepared for the first half hour of "Saving Private Ryan." It was the most graphic portrayal of the Allied invasion of Normandy during WWII that I had ever seen, in particular, the American sector of Omaha Beach. I leaned over and told my son, as we watched in horror, that if his grandfather hadn't left that beach alive, he wouldn't be sitting there. For the next thirty minutes, we both sat there and cried almost uncontrollably, experiencing vicariously what Deno had lived through. Somehow, both of us now knew him a little better and, as painful as it was, we were both grateful for the experience. My son felt a little more connected to his grandfather and so did I.

Of all the vicarious experiences I have had in this life watching movies, nothing can compare to seeing the film, "The Passion of the Christ". No event, in the history of man on this planet, defines the essence of the relationship between authority and dependency than *this* event nearly 2000 years ago outside the city walls of first century Jerusalem. The word itself, "Passion," tells us the whole of the emotional/relational story of God and man. Only in this relationship will we ever ultimately find resolution to our deepest longings. In St. Augustine's "Book One" of *Confessions,* he says it well: "Our hearts are restless until they find their rest in you."

That doesn't mean, however, that in our quest we don't try everything else from failed relationships, to chemicals, to money, to a search for power. As we will see in the next chapter, this search for power and control, in essence, is what it is all about.

CHAPTER FOUR

It's All About Control

The pieces are all dumped out on our table and we have begun to sort through the jumbled mess to find the edge pieces so that we can at least determine how large the puzzle is and have some concept of how to put the pieces back together. In the last three chapters of this book we have identified three of the borders of this gigantic puzzle called *life.* The top border is labeled Authority/Dependency and is really the key to understanding that at which we are looking. The left border shows us that "Emotions Trump" and without this essential piece, we lack a true understanding of the landscape of which life is made. The right border explains the role and place of expectations, suggesting that "We only get two shots in life" to receive the care and nurture we were born to expect.

The bottom and final border of the puzzle can be summed up simply by saying, "It is all about control": Who's got it and what they are going to do with it? Oh, I know what you're thinking. This simply seems like an elaboration of the first piece about authority and dependency. You, in fact, are correct to the extent that all the pieces after A/D are an extension and elaboration of A/D. And yet, this concept of control strikes at some of the deepest issues of life, warranting additional explanation—issues such as free will, rebellion, faith, pride and (certainly not the least of all) emotional-relational safety.

Control Has Gotten A Bad Name

First let me say that control as a concept has gotten a bad name over the last six thousand or so years of human history. Those mainly responsible for the bad name are those controlling types who have been *in control.* Authoritative, dictatorial, and tyrannical are a few of the adjectives used to describe many of the characters dominating the pages of history (real history, not revised history). The twentieth century, of which most of us have lived at least in part, was full of

41

characters whose lives defined this destructive side of control. From Hitler to Stalin, from Pol Pot to Sadam Hussein, their malicious use of power and control saw the destruction of untold millions of human beings and a legacy of cultural chaos for generations yet to come.

Let's bring it down from the lofty heights of history, however, to the everyday lives each of us leads. When have you ever heard the term "controlling" used as a compliment to someone's character? When was the last time you thought of manipulation as a good thing? Probably seldom, if ever. That is because each of us has been on the sharp, receiving edge of the abuse or neglect of control and manipulation. And yet, without someone in control, there is not much good that ever happens.

Take Harold, for example. It seemed to him like a good idea to take his wife out to dinner, a noble attempt to communicate his love and care for her. So how could such good intentions lead to one of the worse fights they had had in months? Things went something like this. At about four o'clock in the afternoon, the husband called home from work and said, "Hey, honey, how would you like to go out for dinner tonight?" She said that it was not necessary. He didn't have to do that. She already had something planned for dinner. He responded by saying that perhaps they could have that meal tomorrow night. Why not get a sitter and have a spontaneous date night? She said, "Okay," and began to rearrange her afternoon and evening, quickly putting herself together for a rendezvous with her man. Dad pulled in the drive to find his date ready for the evening. And so they jumped in the family van. As they were backing out, he said (with all good intentions), "So where would you like to go?" Of course, up until only sixty minutes ago, she had had different plans for supper and her evening. She responded, "I don't know. Where do you want to go?" Although it began with a good idea, *dinner out,* Harold had no clear plan. Out of the husband's passivity, the responsibility for deciding where to go now fell to the wife.

She had accepted that responsibility earlier and planned dinner. Now, when confronted with choosing where to go, that "neglect" place in her was triggered, which caused a slight irritation in her voice when she said, "Why do I always have to decide these things?" He then caught the irritation in her voice, which, in turn, triggered his feelings of hurt and disrespect and responded, "You are always saying that I never take you out on a date!" The word *date* came with added emphasis and was used almost as a four-letter word.

The evening deteriorated from there and, not only was there no spontaneous date night, there wasn't any dinner at all. He ended up pulling the van back into the garage and, when getting out, slamming the van door. She went to their bedroom and cried. Both spent the evening muttering about how nothing ever changes.

You see, it *is* all about control. It was a good thing when the husband took control to shape a spontaneous evening. It all ended, however, when he gave the control and the responsibility to his wife. She was now caught in the middle of her own plans and his plans and expectations for the evening. Even these seemingly small interactions, where no one is really in control, can cause relational disasters. In the previous example, as long as someone was clearly in control, the evening had potential. As soon as the locus of control got blurred, bad things began to happen relationally.

Will *They* Act In My Best Interest?

The big question always is, "Is that person in control going to act in my best interest? And will my desires and wishes be respected in the process?" If I am not convinced that this is the case, then I have to act *in my own* best interest. Acting in our own best interest can look like anything from outright rebellion to a total shut down and withdrawal. And remember: most of this goes on beyond our level of awareness. But, mark my words, when any of our negative emotions are triggered (at any level of awareness) it feels like a loss of control.

Life Seems So Random

Much of it has to do with the perceived, capricious nature of circumstance. Life, to many, seems like random, chance happenings beyond anyone's control. This would include the families into which we are born, the culture, the time in history, the geographical location and any number of factors that impact our lives for better or for worse. We come to believe we are at the mercy and whim of factors that are way beyond our control. The idea that any of us has a free will to choose and, in effect, control anything in our lives is beyond the imaginations of billions of people who have inhabited this planet since the dawn of history.

A couple of years ago, I spent some time in Ukraine, approximately thirteen years after they had broken away from the old Soviet Union. From the clothes I wore, it was probably obvious that I was an American. One evening, as I walked through the subway below Kharkov, Ukraine, I encountered one of the many wandering musicians who play his instrument for the passers-by, hoping for some change to be dropped into his instrument case. As I approached, he began to play on his violin, "The Star Spangled Banner". This was followed by a few more American, patriotic tunes, and then ended with "Strangers in the Night." He boarded the train with us, continuing to play tunes familiar to most Americans. It was actually a memorable and enjoyable experience.

I remember turning to my Ukrainian interpreter and asking if it was that obvious that I was American. Was it the clothes I wore? His response fascinated me. He said that even if I had done everything possible to look like a local, just the way I walked would have identified me as an American. Somewhat amused I asked, "So, just how does an American walk?" He said that I walked like a person who had a history of two hundred years of freedom. Evidently, our beliefs about ourselves are evidenced even in the way we walk.

Freedom's Treasure

Those of us who have experienced the freedoms to choose and to express (through our own free will) will have come to certain beliefs about the world in which we live. Those who founded our country, our rule of law, and in essence the American culture, believed in freedom. They embraced the freedom to choose for ourselves the lives we wanted to live. We also were to choose those in authority over us in order to assure ourselves that they would be individuals who would act in our best interest. Freedom is an awesome treasure that, perhaps, most Americans take for granted.

Even with all the freedoms we enjoy, we often forget that freedom (like gravity) has limits and operates on a knowable set of rules. Consequently, one thing we are never free from is a value system. Just as someone is always in control, that someone has a value system. I have heard it said many times that you cannot legislate morality, meaning that making a law does not affect a person's value system. This, of course, is not true. Laws do affect our value systems. It is not whether or not one can legislate morality, but rather whose morality will be legislated.

Freedom's Boundaries

We are also not free from our own beliefs about ourselves or our beliefs about those in authority. These beliefs are often shaped very
early in life. How many people marry someone thinking that after
sufficient time merely his/her presence and love will change the
other's beliefs, only to find that the authority of the spouse's belief
system is extremely powerful? I am often reminded of those com-
passionate parents who adopt someone else's child thinking that
love will conquer all. They later find, however, that the belief system of that little one is already deeply entrenched in his/her soul.

I am reminded of a young man who, after twenty plus years of
being controlled by his parents, sat in my office having difficulty believing that he still possessed any will of his own. It wasn't that his
parents didn't love him. They did. In fact, so much so that they
couldn't allow him to fail or make any mistake that would have
"long term" harmful effects. As it turned out, the parent's belief systems kept them in fear and anxiety, causing a parenting style that
stifled their son's ability to exert his own will. The young man once
reported, "If I am going to have any success in this life, it will be because I will have been dragged there kicking and screaming by my
parents." In this case, the definition of success is, of course, his parent's definition.

Pride-Motivated Rebellion

Perhaps it would be helpful at this time to address evil and pride-
motivated rebellion. These two factors have played a prominent
role in human history and muddied the waters in our understanding of control. Are there really bad guys or malevolent forces bent
on controlling us for their own selfish and malicious ends? Is there
a real satan roaming the earth seeking whom he may devour . . . a
being who is all about killing, stealing, and destroying?

From the Biblical worldview, which I espouse, the answer is yes,
absolutely. As a matter of fact, the history of mankind is the story of
our (mankind's) freely choosing to join satan's rebellion out of our own
prideful natures. I am defining pride here as *the desire to exalt ourselves above the ultimate authority, God, who Himself is responsible for
our existence.* Satan thought himself equal with God and wanted to
usurp His throne, which prompted his rebellion. We all have the
same choice. Some who make this choice come to embody all that is

evil and are contemptuous of all that God has created. All generations since the dawn of time have struggled with and against the problem of evil. None of us are exempt. Evil operates with a clear understanding that it is all about control. And the prize is the human soul, for in it resides the intellect, the will, and the emotions. This battle for the souls of men has been raging for thousands of years and continues today.

Pride-motivated rebellion seeks to exalt itself; survival-motivated rebellion, however, has a different face. It is an attempt to survive abusive- or neglectful-applied authority. Remember: someone or something is always in control. The application of benevolent power and control, by someone or something in authority does not (for all intents and purposes) breed rebellion. The exception, of course, is the prideful malevolence which, like it or not, comes with the free-will package.

When Adam walked with God in the garden, God was in control, exercising benevolent authority over His creation and delegating some of that authority to Adam. He told Adam to be fruitful, to multiply, to fill the earth and to subdue it. I often wonder what it must have been like to walk with God in the garden and to experience total security and safety. Yes, emotions were a necessity to assist Adam in experiencing the depths of awe and wonder at the beauty of the world in which he found himself. These emotions were especially evident when he was presented with the ultimate in beauty and perfection in all of creation, woman.

In choosing to join satan's rebellion, however, like satan, Adam was cut off from the security and safety of direct dependence on the creator of the universe. And as satan was cast out of Heaven, Adam was cast out of the garden. Thereafter, his safety was *not* assured. From the friendly confines of the garden, Adam and Eve were confronted with a new world that not only failed to provide for their safety, but also (in essence) actually threatened their survival. It was a harsh, cruel world they faced. Further, even the animals that Adam had been commissioned to name now treated these humans as threats to *their* existence.

The Soul Comes To Dominate the System

How was man/Adam to survive? The negative emotions, which heretofore had been only a small part of the human soul, now rose to assume a place of almost unrestrained power in order to facilitate man's survival in this harsh and cruel world. Now there were threats at every turn. Adam and Eve must have struggled with overwhelming fear. Frustrations and hurts entered their existence, resulting in anger. The fig leaves evidenced the guilt and shame they felt as a result of their sin, and (eventually) the sadness and grief they experienced at the loss of their son, Abel.

Now, if they were to survive, their emotions must rule where their spirits had ruled in the time they walked with God. They soon learned that there are natural and spiritual powers with which to be reckoned and they, Adam and Eve, were *not* in control. Being fruitful and multiplying was certainly doable, but subduing was a totally different matter. Their free will (having chosen rebellion) now entered a struggle to survive all the malevolent forces of nature, the spirit world and (perhaps the most dangerous force of all) the wickedness of the human heart.

Estranged But Not Cut Off

Although now estranged from the creator, we have never been completely cut off, forsaken, or abandoned. God's intent from the beginning has been for relationship and blessing. History is the story, after the fall, of God's reconciling the world to Himself.

With all the forces arrayed against us, striving to usurp control, it is no wonder that we forget that there ever was benevolent authority, using its power and control in *our* best interest. Consequently, consciously (but more often unconsciously) we decide that we can *only* control ourselves, and later find we often lack success at this as well. Again, all of our survival styles are initiated mostly unconsciously in order to facilitate a sense of control and safety.

That is why the chickens act crazy. They feel *out of control.*

Also remember that the most significant authority/dependency relationship in our lives is that first one: the relationship we had with our parents or caretakers. Suppose they didn't have good parents either, and so on, and so on, up the family tree? These are the people who are in control of our lives, at least until we mature enough physically and emotionally to actually take control of our own lives. How many of us are the recipients of generations of family dysfunction, experientially and genetically?

Not Enough Love

Remember, too, about our expectation of care. We have an idea, somewhere deep in our souls, that the people in control are supposed to love and care for us. But, as I may have mentioned, it has been my observation that there is not enough love in this world . . . consequently, not enough care . . . and, consequently, an entire planet full of folks with issues. For so many of us, being in control becomes a substitute for being loved. For others, being in control means staying safe. It is entirely possible, however, to be in control and still be unsafe.

I know what you're thinking. I get the picture about it being all about control. But if I don't feel that I have it, how do I get it? Do I have to fight or rebel? If so much of this goes on outside of my awareness, where do I even begin?

Beliefs About Control

As much as you may not want to hear this, it really begins in our minds; that is, in our beliefs about control. Is the locus of control external or internal? Are we, in fact, subject to the whims of circumstance? There is no question that circumstance plays a major role in our lives. The question remains, however, are we controlled from without or within? Do we believe that control is a good thing or a bad thing? Do we have a free will or has it been usurped? And, since emotions trump, are we inevitably at their mercy? Is it not better, at the very least, to have some emotions (regardless of the locus of control) than to go through life as some sort of walking zombie?

In his book, *Emotional Intelligence,* Goleman suggests that our ability to achieve any measure of success is not, as it turns out, related to IQ, Intelligence Quotient. In reality, it is determined by EQ, Emotional Quotient. He further suggests that the success predictors can be detected and taught at a very early age.

EQ & The Marshmallow Test

The success predictor I refer to is called the marshmallow test and it goes something like this. Sit your three, four, or five-year-old child down at a table and set a marshmallow in front of her/him. Tell her/him that the marshmallow is hers/his to eat any time she/he chooses. If he/she will wait for you to return before eating the marshmallow, then you will give her/him a second one. Wait ten minutes or so, but be sure to return with the second marshmallow. To not return with the second marshmallow would launch another whole set of dynamics related to the abuse and neglect of authority. That's it. That is all there is to the test. If the child can wait for the second marshmallow, his/her chance for success in adult life is greatly enhanced.

Emotional Control

You see, it is all about emotional control. Whatever that child has to do in order to control those trumping emotions will facilitate his/her ability to delay gratification. The trumping emotions beckon him/her to eat it now. Who cares about another one? Or perhaps, he/she hears, "Eat it now. They're never coming back anyway." This is why it is imperative that you return with the second marshmallow. There has to be a reason for self-discipline. Hope deferred makes the heart sick. (Proverbs 13:12)

In order to be in control of our emotions, we have to be in touch with them. The common myth here is that emotions are best controlled by denial, repression, and suppression. In other words, stuff those bothersome or painful emotions as far down or away from our awareness as we can. Without over-generalizing here, it seems men are better at this than women. Seemingly held in high esteem in movies and fiction is the prototypical male who remains unemotional and totally in control in the face of pain and danger.

Oblivion Scale

This level of control, however, can lead to serious emotional/relational disconnections. I call it the "oblivion scale." For weeks, months, and sometimes years, I "lay it out," telling a couple that emotions trump and that, in order to connect at a meaningful level, they must be willing to experience the emotions. They say that they believe what I'm saying. But believing it is one thing; understanding and applying it is quite another. It is actually painful to watch as the husband, at some level, becomes aware that his spouse (whom he also loves at some level) has become angry, bitter, and finally cold and distant. She responds in this way in an effort to survive his inability to connect at any meaningful emotional level. (While in my counseling experience, I *have* worked with wives who are measurably high on the "oblivion scale," I have found this dysfunction to primarily be a male malady.)

Safety First

The male in the couple described above thought it was about the money, or the kids, or sex, or the catchall diagnosis, "inability to communicate." No, in reality, it was his inability to connect with her at that deep emotional place in her soul. Fail at this and you do so at your own relational peril. Carl Rogers calls it "psychological safety" and defines it as unconditional positive regard with the absence of evaluation and with an empathetic understanding. This is a place where one can *feel* safe. It must, however, be communicated emotionally. Communication at this level is not an intellectual exercise. Just saying the words does not get it done relationally.

Being in touch with one's emotions is just the first step in the process. But, in reality, it is not all that complex either. Once in touch with what we are feeling, we now have the opportunity to get our intellects involved in the process. We can ask ourselves, how do I feel about how I am feeling? Is what I am feeling rational or irrational? Is what I am feeling appropriate or out of proportion to the situation? Am I feeling angry when I really am afraid, or am I feeling guilty when I really need to give myself permission to be angry?

Pain & Emotional Defenses

Remember that negative emotions are uncomfortable at best and, at worst, can be debilitating and painful. Our emotional defense mechanisms or styles kick in to keep the pain in check. Often we are only aware of what happened after the defenses have kicked in. Then the information we need from our true feelings gets lost somewhere in that vast landscape of the soul. We do or say things in this state of oblivion and can't understand why we receive the reactions we do. It is like a double whammy: our emotions trump, our defenses kick in, and we think we know what is happening. In reality, we are oblivious. But, if anyone questions our oblivion, a whole new round of relational disconnections is set off. Sound too far-fetched? Ask yourself just how connected you are to significant people in your life. Or how well you relate to the cashier at the grocery or your co-workers on the job. Consider your relationship with the person who whips in ahead of you and takes your parking spot, in particular.

Managing Our Feelings vs. Suppressing or Denying Them

Once we give ourselves the opportunity to feel what we are feeling and can engage our rational intellect enough to have *feelings about* our feelings, we are now in a position to control or, if you prefer, manage our emotions. If we deny our feelings or suppress them, they will come out sideways in sarcasm, distancing or even placating. Of course, we could just let them fly. In every case, the relational consequences are usually disastrous. We lose the intimacy and care we long for and can't understand why life is so hard. We feel totally out of control and at the whim of people and circumstance.

Often individuals ask the question, "How will I know when and if I am getting emotionally healthy?" Remember, it is a rough ole world and bad things do happen. Our emotions will get triggered. Just as with the physical body, one measure of health is how quickly we are able to recover. Does it take us an hour, a day, or months to recover from emotionally painful events? The answer here is the quicker the better. The key is to be in touch with and make good decisions in managing our emotions. I remember once hearing the story of an otherwise emotionally healthy man who had a devastating emotional setback. As a result, for the next ten years, he shut down and became a literal hermit in his apartment, losing relationship with his wife and kids. Ten years is a long time to live under the tyranny of trumping emotions.

Managing Others Emotions

It doesn't, however, stop there. Once getting to the place of emotional self-control, we are now in the position to learn how to manage the emotions of other people. I know what you are thinking. Managing or controlling someone else's emotions sounds like a bad thing. Having been the victims of emotional manipulation, control, and abuse, we do not want to now become the perpetrators. As I said earlier, it is those controlling and abusive manipulators that give control and manipulation a bad name.

Managing or controlling someone else's emotions is really the core piece when we speak of it being all about control. Throughout history it has been those who have had a working knowledge of the human soul and how to influence its emotional decision-making that have prospered, for good or evil. When one begins to understand the workings of the soul, starting with his/her own soul and then another's soul, he/she will begin to feel a sense of control and well-being.

Culturally Damaged Souls

There are peoples and cultures that have lived under tyranny and neglect for generations and even centuries. The souls of these people come to see the world differently than those of us who have had two-hundred-plus years of freedom. Even in this country, there have been many people groups who have lived under oppression—from the black slaves of the South to the Appalachian folk of the Cumberland Plateau. When a people group lives disadvantaged for several generations, they begin to think and see the world differently. In my years as a social worker, I encountered what has been labeled a "welfare mentality." Call it what you will, great fear resides in the souls of a people who for generations have lived feeling no sense of control.

Emotional/Relational Beliefs Can Equal Beliefs About God

Many of these emotional/relational beliefs are translated into individual biblical doctrines and beliefs about God. What *feels* true is usually what we *believe* to be true which was the case with Betty. She said she was done. For forty years of her life, she had been a pleaser. It was Betty's way of surviving the dysfunctional families into which she was born and into which she later married. It is not unusual for an individual to choose a husband or wife much like his/her own father or mother. Subconsciously we reason that, if we can change him/her, we will resolve our old, deep emotional issues. This is precisely what this "pleaser" had done for twenty plus years with an angry father and almost twenty years with an angry husband. Now she was *done* with her placating/pleasing defense style that was intended to keep her safe. It hadn't kept her safe. Consequently, she was in a lot of pain and *done*. She said to me, "From now on, I am only going to try to please God." I said, "Please, don't do that. You will just be trying to relate to God as you have tried to relate to your father and your husband. He is really not much like either one of them."

Our creator has given us a free will. Within the exercise of our free will is the essence of freedom. To take control of our own will is what our creator expected when He gave us free will. Many tyrants in the history of the world (from dictators to parents) would have us believe that our wills should be subject to theirs. They create and impose closed systems that operate on fear or shame.

How many people in the last six thousand years have lived their lives based in such a belief system?

Nothing Good Happens Unless *Someone* Is In Control

Nothing good ever really happens until control is taken. But, therein lies the rub. What we choose to *do* with the control is equally important. For while we have freedom, we are never free from a value system, beliefs about ourselves, or beliefs on authority. Do we believe the one in authority will act in our best interest, not abusing or neglecting us? If not, how do we assure ourselves of care? Sometimes all we want is to merely regain, or perhaps gain for the first time, some sense of equal power in relationship. This can necessarily be a very fluid situation as we attempt to take and maintain a sense of control, especially with controlling people.

The fighting and bickering had gone on for a couple of years. The couple in my office had finally realized that they could not resolve this situation themselves. They needed help. They needed counseling. That didn't stop them, however, from continuing the battle in my office during the early months of counsel. I usually allow this to go on for a period of time, and then point out the futility of the couple's current strategy to fix their marriage. Most people believe that if they simply point out the bad or counterproductive behaviors in the other, that their partner will hear the complaint and adjust his/her behavior accordingly, especially if it's said with a sharp edge. This strategy, founded on a faulty emotional/relational belief, dies hard. So they battled on, expecting and appealing to me to judge the worthiness of their individual complaints, continuing in their beliefs that they merely needed to learn how to better communicate.

When finally and sufficiently wrought out, I returned them to the concept that *it is all about control.* In this case, the wife was the controller with a petulant demeanor and sharp tongue. The husband, being accustomed to similar behaviors in his mother, had now (after forty plus years) decided to fight. With control threatened and the relational stakes high, the hostilities escalated. And finally, after so many years of bickering, they had forgotten why the fight had begun in the first place.

What had started the fight was really not within either's control. Circumstances had conspired against them, creating an increasingly chaotic family life. The *old relational deal:* control on the part of the wife and passivity on the part of the husband was taxed beyond what their co-dependent, dysfunctional relationship could survive. As it turned out, the wife's control was actually an emotional, defense style designed to insure that she would never be neglected or abandoned like she had been in childhood by her father and, later, by her first husband. This defense style was based on the belief that if she were to stay in control, then bad things would not happen. As it is with most defense styles, her *defense style* had become the problem in and of itself and had caused bad relational things to happen.

Abuse/Neglect Create Vulnerability

When people are abused and neglected, they enter a state of vulnerability, meaning that anyone so inclined may take advantage of them for their own selfish, and often evil, purposes. If this happens during childhood, when they haven't yet developed critical thinking skills, they are vulnerable to the lies and distortions those in authority (willingly or unwillingly) create in their minds. Evil, knowing this, whether manifested through the devil himself or through a selfish heart, will use it to its advantage by creating chaos and instability. When the time is right, evil will present itself as the only true solution. Remember, whoever is creating the chaos is ultimately in control. Even children know this. The ones willing to make a mess will, knowingly or unknowingly, make a bigger mess to get themselves out of trouble. For, you see, the enemy of us all, whether it is our families, our institutions, our governments or our cultures, is chaos and instability. We need the rules and accountability to stay safe. When the rules cease to maintain control or become controlling, our emotional and/or physical survival is triggered, creating fear, anger, or shame. Our emotional pain must be addressed or we go crazy. This is precisely what happens when there is a fox in the chicken coop.

CHAPTER FIVE

Relational Rule Number One

Now you have a sense of the size and shape of this puzzle called "life." The top border is the core concept of *Authority/Dependency*; the two side borders are *Emotions Trump* and *Expectations*; and the bottom border is *It's All About Control.*

When putting together a jigsaw puzzle, if you are like me, you take a look at the picture on the front of the puzzle box when you are ready to fill in the body of the puzzle. Dominating the landscape of the picture of our puzzle of life is a huge cloud and mist-covered mountain that seems both awesome and mysterious but also evokes a sense of foreboding.

In the grand scheme of life, this mysterious mountain is what I call "Relational Rule Number One." Next you will see why for thousands of years of human history, it has been and continues to be shrouded in mist and mystery.

Relational Rule Number One simply states that whoever is in the position of authority initiates and shapes the quality of relationship and is responsible for it.

That 's it. At first glance, it seems fairly simple, straightforward and obvious. Wouldn't you agree? But, at second glance, the mist and clouds begin to gather. What seemed so simple and straightforward before isn't as obvious now. As it turns out, for all the thousands of years of human history that have been recorded, those in authority have been going about the business of convincing those in the position of dependency that they, the D's, are in fact responsible for the quality of relationship.

Violations of Relational Rule # 1

The violations of Relational Rule Number One come in many shapes and sizes and rely heavily on fear through intimidation or guilt and shame-based authority. All violations are related to the abuse and/or neglect of authority. Year after year of violations of Relational Rule Number One by those in authority results with those in positions of dependency feeling and believing that there absolutely must be *something wrong with them.* Big people don't make mistakes or do bad things. Do they? No, they reason, "the bad" must be in them. This often begins a lifetime of self-hatred. Much of what I do in counseling is primarily an attempt to help people accept and deal with the fact that for six thousand years, the world's authority systems have been totally violating Relational Rule Number One.

I know what you are thinking: grand schemes of life; thousands of years of history; mist and mystery. It sounds like a big dramatization and an over-simplification of the complexities of life. Even if that is *not* what you are thinking right now, it certainly was what I thought. Day in and day out, I saw this pattern play out in story after story of those who came for counseling, hoping to deal with their issues and pain. In the telling of their stories, these individuals revealed deeply held beliefs about themselves that seemed impervious to truth or to change. You don't have to be in counseling to understand that these emotionally-charged beliefs cut to the core perception of his/her own value. These beliefs determine, in fact, the quality of our relationships for a lifetime or until we finally hear the truth from God Himself about whom we really are. He alone was responsible for our creation. And so, from where did these beliefs come and why are they so powerful?

A Sad History

Remember the history of our first ancestors, Adam and Eve, who walked with God in the garden? They accepted the serpent's deceit and chose to join his rebellion. As a result, they were put out of that place of beauty, protection and provision. The removal from the garden must have been a terrible thing in and of itself, but far, far worse than that was the separation from the Alpha and the Omega, the Love and the Light of the universe, the creator of life. The separation, however, was not a total separation. They were never disowned or forsaken. No, they were left to sort things out under the influence of the one who embodies darkness and deceit, the one with whom they had chosen to side.

God has never left us without a witness of Himself. The truth has always been there to be discovered. But the lies and deception are powerful. Don't think that if it had been you or me in the garden that we would have chosen any differently. As I am about to show you, we believed and acted on the same lies for thousands of years and taught them to our children as well.

Something Is Out There

Somewhere deep in our souls, we have the belief that there really is something out there directing the universe, influencing circumstance and history. We further believe that it is up to us to figure out how to get "it" on our side or, at least, willing to be influenced by what we think or do. Throughout history, literally billions of people have come to believe that this something is a spirit not of human origin or make-up, but far more powerful and demanding. Religion, as we know it, is the process of coming to know what this powerful, spiritual being wants from us and carefully making sure that we comply. It is what I call "placating the gods" (small "g"). If we accomplish this without causing anger, perhaps bad things won't happen. Jesus, by the way, never came to this earth to establish a religion. He came to re-establish relationship with us and to proclaim that the Kingdom of God (designed for relationship and blessing) has come to us.

Science and Reason

The truth is that there really are powerful, spiritual beings *out there.* We have spent the last four or five hundred years in western culture becoming "enlightened," meaning that with the advent of science and reason we can explain nearly all the mysteries of life. We can reassure ourselves that what goes bump in the night can be explained by science. There is no reason to fear anything except, of course, our own selfish interests which have caused all the bad things in this world from war to global warming.

It seems that the more we learn from science and reason, however, the more questions we have and the less we seem to really know for sure. It really does seem that what we thought we had *nailed down* is coming loose. We (in the western world) have shown greater interest and nearly preoccupation with the "paranormal" than ever before. If Hollywood's futuristic movies are any indication of our beliefs about the future, then there are few who think the world is going to get much better.

Placating the Gods

"Placating" is an attempt to please that which we believe to have power and control over us, so that we will not be abused or neglected. The message sent by one in authority is that if you think and/or act correctly, then he/she, who has the power and control, will be more inclined to provide the needed and expected care. If we, in our position of dependency, however, fail to think and/or act correctly, then the one in authority, of course, has no choice but to punish us or withhold the needed care. And just to keep us guessing, there seems to be only minimal apparent correlation between our acts of pleasing and the resulting provisions of care. We may act and think correctly for days. Then we commit one transgression and it is as if we had never done anything right. The punishment is out of proportion, rarely fitting the offense. We come to truly believe that the powers that be are capricious and petulant, unknowable and unfair.

You can see that we easily and logically conclude that (as D's) we have to become responsible for our own survival, both physical and emotional. As someone once told me, "That's just the way of it. So get used to it because nothing has changed in the last six thousand years. If you have a problem with that, it is your problem. You need to just *get over it.*" I spoke about the get-over-it type of thinking earlier in Chapter Two.

If you don't like the words "placating" or "pleasing," then substitute the words "performance" or "perfectionism." These attempts of *obedience* of sorts are activities that those in the position of dependency believe they have to do in order to survive. Some ultimately rebel against the abuse and neglect and pay the price for their freedom. Others come to believe that they cannot assert their own will and, consequently, assume a lifetime of dependency. There are those who believe that suffering should be a way of life, a passive resistance to the spiritual powers of darkness (both without and within the human soul).

The D's Are Responsible

The message given then by authority is that the *quality of relationship* is dependent not on whomever is in authority, but rather on whomever is in the position of dependency. Whenever this is the case, it is clearly a violation of Relational Rule Number One. The "D" *cannot* initiate or shape the quality of relationship no matter how committed the "A" is in convincing him/her otherwise. When we are children, we have no ability to critically understand relationships with authority. The messages and training we receive are taken at face value. They are adopted as core values and beliefs and are carried in our souls for the rest of our lives.

While it is true that somewhere deep inside our souls we sense that something is wrong; it is virtually impossible for us (as children) to conceive of big people being wrong or making mistakes, especially since apologies are so rare. Who among us can admit that we are not good parents or that our parents were not very good parents either. And so, the lies and dysfunction, the abuse and neglect continue from generation to generation. Eventually no one remembers that it could or should be any different. Yet the longing for it *to be different* remains. Deep inside all of us is the longing to return to paradise, to the place of Relational Rule Number One, where under the benevolence of our creator, we live without fear and anxiety, without being driven by anger and rage or guilt and shame.

The situation is parallel to the one for which a computer programmer is hired to create a sophisticated program, perhaps, the security of a bank or corporation. The set of firewalls or defenses are so complex that it is virtually impossible to convince the program to allow you entrance. Yes, there are levels of penetration built into the program to facilitate the daily transactions needed to do business. The largest assets, however, are kept locked deeply away. The programmer has programmed in a secret backdoor password that only she/he knows. He/she merely types in the password and, like magic, he/she is in. A parent actually does the same through his/her secret password by conveying the message that it is *you who* are responsible for your own care, not him/her. If you fail, he/she will criticize, punish, and/or reject you.

Fast-forward a few years from your toddler years to your school years and the scene is the same. This pattern of dysfunction continues on into the work place and, even in marriage, the message doesn't change. The person in authority reiterates, "I can't love you, protect you, support and affirm you. I can't do my job as your authority because you break the rules and/or act badly. In fact, perhaps there really *is* something wrong with you."

There Really Is Something Wrong With Me

Once someone is convinced that this is true, it is very difficult to convince him or her otherwise. Not reason or logic, not even love and compassion can penetrate this belief. He/She may spend the rest of his/her life to their own detriment, convincing others that there really is something wrong with them. They develop a deep, raging hatred that the world will most assuredly pay for in the destruction they perpetrate. There are also those we call "high maintenance" who seem to constantly need reassurance that they are okay and that what they believe about themselves isn't true.

It gets very tricky here because by now there really is something wrong with them. They believe a lie, which is very painful and creates a lot of conflict in the soul. We call it low self-image and, of course, it is. Never forget, however, that this understanding comes in relationship to the abuse and/or neglect of authority.

God's No Different . . . . . Right?

All that I have described gets projected onto God. He is the ultimate authority. Although we can't have a face to face conversation to find out exactly what we are supposed to do, we do have the Ten Commandments and the knowledge that if we transgress one of them, then He has no choice but to punish us by causing bad things to happen. If we don't balance up the ledger by doing good deeds, then He may have no choice but to condemn us to the place of eternal punishment, hell.

What I am suggesting to you is that the initiation and shaping of the quality of the relationship between whoever is in the position of authority and those who are dependent and under that authority is the responsibility of the "A," not the "D." This includes all authority from parents to teachers, from police to judges, from priests to bosses and, especially, God Himself. *I* didn't create Relational Rule Number One. God did! None of us create truth. We only discover it, you see, because *He* made this world the way it is.

60

Picture yourself on the first day of a new job. Instead of reviewing the normal information found in job descriptions and employee manuals, such as start times, bathroom breaks and so on, your supervisor chooses to sit down next to you with two cups of fresh coffee (which just happens to be your personal favorite, Starbuck's French Roast). He/She looks at you and begins the conversation with how fortunate they feel that you have chosen to work with them. They feel that given the gifts and talents they observe in you that the job you are about to begin will be both challenging and rewarding. They also want you to know that you are free to take initiative and be creative in shaping the position (as you see fit) in order to fulfill the tasks and responsibilities ahead. Further, they want to assure you that they are there to support and affirm you in your new adventure. They understand that their job is to provide you with all the tools and resources you will need to "get it done."

The Violation Now the Norm

Most people laugh, when I suggest this scenario, at how ridiculous it seems. Some suggest (in no uncertain terms) that my account is from a fantasy world. In other words, I am not dealing with reality. Others have told me that they actually did get that speech where they work. The only problem was that it was just a speech. In the day-to-day work life, it really didn't work that way. You may now see that for thousands of years, the violations of Relational Rule Number One are the norm. Anything approaching the actual application of the rule sounds like a fantasy created in my own mind. But it isn't a fantasy. It was God's original intent when He created us. The enemy planted the insidious lie. We now accept the lie as reality and as truth about our ultimate authority.

The Ultimate Fox In the Chicken Coop

There is no doubt that there *is* a fox in this chicken coop called earth, and he is extremely clever and deceptive. He has no intention of allowing you to gain any inkling of the truth. He knows that when you hear the truth, you may choose differently than your first ancestors. In order to maintain the lie, it is important for satan to usurp and co-opt human positions of power. This is easily done because the evil one does have power himself. Satan is not, however, all-powerful. Although he tried, he could not usurp God's throne. But, as evidenced by history's spiritual mediums, shamans and sorcerers, he does parcel out real power to those who would do his biding, including those able to assume positions of political, cultural or religious power. When one of these individuals, corrupted by the lie and drunk with power, assumes control of a tribe or people group that has been left vulnerable by the harshness of life, the inevitable carnage is recorded in the historical accounts of human life and culture.

Religious systems are not exempt. Administered by fallen man as the result of pride, they fall prey to the same corruption that all systems do. One significant distinction, however, is that the final betrayal is so much more painful because religious systems represent the creator and ultimate authority. For example, religious legalism is itself a violation of Relational Rule Number One. By rigorously holding adherents to strict standards *(Don't break the rules!)* and seeking to prohibit them from a "lifeline" connection to their creator (insisting on the need for intermediaries), they usurp a position of power and wield that power in ways that even our creator Himself does not. That is why God Himself, at the moment of Christ's Passion, tore the curtain to the Holy of Holies from top to bottom saying, in effect, "All of you may come *directly* to Me. Your sins have been covered. There is no need for any intermediaries. Just as it was in the garden, you can walk with and talk with me directly."

Satan's Efforts Directed At the World's Authority Systems

With that act, the ultimate fate of the enemy was sealed, but not executed. He was still free to roam the earth, seeking whom he may devour. But, for the most part, he does not focus on individuals. Rather he concentrates his efforts on the authority systems of this world. At the center of his plan is the destruction of God's first created institution, the family. The first focus of every and all of the destructive religious, governmental, and ideological systems is the systematic breaking of the bond between husband and wife and between parent and child.

You see, satan must first convince parents to violate Relational Rule Number One. Parents then convince their totally dependent and vulnerable little ones of the violation, who then become fearful, shameful, or full of rage. Then these little ones, carrying into adulthood the belief in the lie, become putty in the hands of any and all that would use them for their own selfish and often malicious ends. Urging them to greater and greater sacrifice in order to receive the expected care or even convincing them that only the sacrifice of their own lives for the greater good of the cause will make a way for their own children to finally receive the expected care. It doesn't matter to satan if these authority systems are cultural, governmental, religious or corporate; any authority system will do.

Our Only Hope

When all authority systems having control over an individual agree in perpetuating the lie, then one feels trapped and hopeless. Only in the actual understanding and relationship with the creator is there hope. This is why, historically, all totalitarian systems are closed systems. No one is allowed in or out. A belief in the God of the Bible is forbidden.

You may now understand how violations of Relational Rule Number One by all authority systems can make most of us feel as if we are living in one big chicken coop with one fox after another. One additional piece, the concept of responsibility, can also get a little "sticky." As stated in Relational Rule Number One, those in the position of authority are responsible for the quality of relationship, which is especially important when bad things happen. Confusion results when we equate responsibility with blame. When bad things happen (and they often do) it is a natural thing to assess blame in an attempt to find some cause-and-effect relationship. Once finding the cause, we then feel a greater sense of control over the next bad thing that may happen.

Responsibility Does Not Equal Blame

The problem is that cause and effect are not so easily discerned. It is not unusual for us to accept simple answers for complex causes. For example, I am having a bad day because I am under spiritual attack. Maybe. Maybe not. Or we look for complex reasons and resolutions when the simple ones will do. A favorite illustration of mine is the structural steel engineer who was called in to extricate a semi truck that had become stuck beneath a low, overhead bridge. It was the ten-year-old bystander who suggested that they let some air out of the tires.

In order to understand responsibility in the context of Relational Rule Number One, we must first agree that responsibility is *not* the same as blame. For most of us, however, they seem synonymous. That perception chills most individuals in positions of authority from taking any responsibility at all. So when something bad happens, we often respond, "Cover your rear ASAP," rather than, "Okay, bad things have happened. I accept responsibility. Now how can I use my authority to fix this?"

One of the most touching examples I have heard of an individual in authority accepting responsibility (although he was not to blame for bad things happening) comes from WWII. The story was told to me by a friend whose father was a gunny sergeant in the Marines Corps during the fight for Iwo Jima. All of her life, the only father she knew was the disabled veteran who had suffered a debilitating wound in the war. During a particular intense firefight, he (along with other marines) was pinned down in a foxhole. In order to save their lives and the lives of others, he ordered a fellow marine to lay down cover fire so that they could change positions. This strategy was an effort to outflank the enemy position. The assignment was a dangerous one and the other marine momentarily froze, putting all in jeopardy. In that split second, the gunny accepted the responsibility for all and took up the position to lay down the cover fire. And in that moment, he took a bullet in the hip, causing him to be disabled for the rest of his life. I asked my friend if she ever heard her father complain about either the other soldier or the cause of his own disability. Her answer: "No, not once."

Responsibility Rolls Downhill

The non-acceptance of responsibility by authority has many faces including intimidation, shame, rejection, manipulation, belittling, and the lack of provision, protection, support, or affirmation. Just because some in authority choose not to accept responsibility does not mean that it ceases to exist. Responsibility is an essential and key component of relationship. What happens when authority does not accept responsibility is that responsibility rolls downhill from the A to the D. When this happens, it is hard to describe just how badly the D is made to feel. As a matter of fact, "bad" does not begin to express the feeling. It is in this relational transaction that the message is conveyed: "There is something wrong with you." This is why it simply doesn't matter on which side of the A/D equation you find yourself. Just having an A/D relational event will trigger your issues, as you will see in the following illustration.

A young girl was raised by a single mother and given the responsibility of caring for her younger siblings. Mom had to work three jobs and was seldom home. Fast-forward this girl's life ten years later to her fifth year of marriage. She and her husband come for counseling with the presenting problems: a lack of communication and intimacy issues. The husband tries to describe the situation by saying, "If I didn't know better, I would say that she doesn't want to have sex with me because (as crazy as it sounds) she is afraid of having kids. But she loves kids. She teaches kindergarten."

As it turns out, the core of the issue is her resistance to accepting responsibility as a mother. She could accept responsibility for other people's kids as a teacher, but the thought of having responsibility for her own felt (and there is that word), "bad." Although now on the opposite side of the A/D equation, this woman's issues were still being triggered. Remember how we look for cause and effect answers? Even if we suppose that the woman in our example was on anti-depressants and anti-anxiety medications, coupled with hormonal treatment for her low libido issues, none of these treatments would address the real issues.

Responsibility & Control

In chapter four, I suggested that it is all about control. Part of being in control is the acceptance of responsibility. It is not unusual at all that many in the position of authority resist taking control because it feels so bad to accept responsibility. "No one ever accepted responsibility for me." "We can only be responsible for ourselves." We live in a time when fathers, who take control and accept responsibility, are in tremendous demand and short supply. When bad things happen in their families, it often doesn't even occur to them that the responsibility may, in fact, be theirs. Rather, we hear such simplistic and seemingly common-sense phrases as, "He made his bed; now he needs to sleep in it," or "She is eighteen now. She is an adult. My job is over," or "It is not my fault." While it may be true that it is not his fault, as a father, it *is* his responsibility.

Personal Responsibility

Those in authority who accept and assume responsibility for their dependents teach responsibility to those dependent on authority. When responsibility is assumed for us, it tells us as D's that it is okay to take personal responsibility for ourselves. One responsibility that a person in authority has is to protect their dependents, sometimes even from themselves. As I mentioned earlier, overindulgence will cause a child to have problems as easily as abuse or neglect. The responsibility to teach and train the moral realities and right value judgments comes with the territory of being in authority. None of us are free from the authority of a value system. We have all adopted one or another. But what value system is in our collective best interest? Religious systems have been problematic for most of human existence. I believe what works best is a relational system based on the Creator's intent for relationship and blessing, where (when bad things happen) *He* accepts responsibility.

God's Responsibility

In the end I am going to suggest that ultimately it is all God's responsibility. He is the ultimate and final authority. If Relational Rule Number One is truth, then one can only conclude that it is He who initiates and shapes the quality of relationship with us. It means that He is responsible for all the bad things that happen. Again, we struggle with Him being *to blame* for all the bad things, i.e. cause and effect. What I am suggesting, however, is that while not to blame, He is nevertheless responsible for fixing it. He has, in fact, done just that. As the Apostle, Paul says, "God showed His love for us in that while we were yet sinners (which means that God accepted the responsibility for all the bad things, sins, that have or ever will happen) Christ died for us" (Rom. 5:8). In that act, He made possible the redemption of all things.

Redemption: A Pipe Dream?

For non-believers, redemption is a pipe dream. All they can hope for is that perhaps through the social, evolutionary process or (at some point) the right application of good laws, good intentions, or scientific findings, we can progress to some state of utopia where we all live in harmony with each other and the physical world, maybe not now, but some day. But for them, there is no redemption, only a hope of higher functioning or the basic good in man ultimately triumphing.

Believers also have a problem with redemption. We see and experience the seeming triumph of evil. It seems that the foxes in the chicken coop are wreaking havoc. There are no Farmer J's to accept responsibility for the abused and neglected. The world appears to be getting darker and darker. That is the way it is with foxes: the closer they get to losing control, the more crazed they become in trying to usurp it. If this world really is coming to a climax, then we can expect the cornered fox to up the ante, primarily by preying on those he has held brainwashed for centuries. Inciting them to greater and greater acts of random, violent abuse, the fox's mission is to terrorize everyone into believing that there is no one who is willing enough to accept responsibility for the defense and protection of our free wills.

Redemption Only In the Hereafter

It even seems that while we believe in the concept of redemption, we live like we believe it only applies to the hereafter. Consequently, any redemption in this life is a fantasy. Can it really be true that the God of the universe heals and restores lives in the here and now? This is exactly what I am suggesting. In my position as a counselor, I have experienced the power of the living God (through His Holy Spirit) heal and restore wounded and damaged lives and relationships. God said He would restore what the locust has eaten (Joel 2:25). I believe that He gives that promise for now, as well as eternity. I will take some time in chapter seven to talk about the concepts of inner healing. Inner healing is for you and it is for now.

The fact remains, though, that the final authority, God Himself, is responsible for the process. He has no problem accepting that responsibility even to the point of sacrificing His son, Jesus, on a Roman cross to provide for this redemption. There are, however, many, many roadblocks when we attempt to connect with the final authority. When we think of engaging in a relational transaction or encountering an authority in any way, our defenses (many times unconsciously) kick in. Perhaps we made an inner vow at a young age that, "I will never allow anyone or any thing to control me." In my psychiatric manual, there are twenty-three defense mechanisms listed which one might choose to deal with this emotional pain. Remember: if it can cause pain, it has some power over me, which puts it in the "A" category. Most, if not all of the A's in our lives, have violated Relational Rule Number One; all, that is, except God Himself.

Religious Deceptions

Is this hard to believe? Well, it is no wonder. For thousands of years, religion (which I define as man's attempt to *work* his way into a positive relationship with God) has been projecting earthly abuse and neglect of authority onto God, trying to convince us that we are the responsible party; that we have to initiate and shape the quality of relationship. Obey the rules; i.e. don't sin or offend the gods in thought or deed. Be pious, pure, holy and ready to sacrifice. And so the list goes on. At this point, you may find yourself adding your own items to the list.

Imagine

Forgive my passion here, but I believe religion and doctrine have turned billions of people over the centuries *away* from receiving His blessing and entering into relationship, a relationship that He had intended from the beginning. It is the violation of Relational Rule Number One that is, in large part, responsible for our human pain and suffering. Imagine a world where fathers understood and applied Relational Rule Number One: where they protected and provided for all those dependent upon them; where they accepted their responsibilities to initiate and shape a quality relationship; where they supported, affirmed and, to the best of their ability, always acted in the "D's" best interest.

Imagine a world where the foxes are not allowed to assume positions of power in any structure or system. The psalmist gives us a glimpse into a world like this, saying, "I have not seen the righteous forsaken, or his descendants begging bread." (Psalm 37:25) Yes, of course, this is a picture of eternity, a return to paradise. But it is also a picture of our world *this side* of eternity when we grasp a core understanding of A/D and apply it, first in our own family and then in our children's. I know we live in a fallen world. Even though I live in probably the freest and safest society in the history of the world, I see and experience the effects almost daily. But, I have hope for us all because of the redemptive power of our creator. It isn't a naïve hope, but a hope born of understanding *why things are the way they are* and experiencing healing and restoration through the Living God.

CHAPTER SIX

Relational Rule Number Two

When I am in the process of explaining Relational Rule Number One, I am invariably interrupted with the question that goes something like, "Okay. I think I understand what you're saying: that whoever is in the position of authority is responsible for the quality of the relationship. But don't I, as the 'D', have some responsibility in the relationship?" This very normal, first response indicates just how successful those in authority have been in convincing the "D's" in this world that the responsibility for relationship is theirs. Of course, there are responsibilities that the "D" assumes in relationship. But we can't even begin to talk about the dependent's part of relationship until the truth of Relational Rule Number One has made it through the maze of beliefs that we have learned and adopted and the cognitive filter through which we perceive life.

Brain Filters & DNA

This "filter" was originally shaped by the biochemical "stuff" called DNA that we inherited at birth from generations past. This would include emotional and spiritual memory as well. This filter was then continually added to by life's experiences from the time we were conceived. Consequently, if we fail to have parents or caretakers who accept their responsibilities for our care, that filter is going to be a *jumbled mess.* Thus, when we are very young, the normal expectations of care begin to wane and responsibility for our own care and survival is assumed. And all of this transpires before we even know the difference between beans and apple butter. Then our survival emotions kick in and dominate our mental/emotional landscape. This often leads us to conclude that life has always been the way it was when we grew up; for, you see, our emotional beliefs were shaped very early. *Our* truth about life will be what truth has always been: that there is no one to care for us, except us. It is asking too much of us to trust in any authority; that is (of course) if we care anything at all about authority in the first place.

Denial Works For Me

I know what you're thinking. You say to yourself, "I've read about abused children and seen the movies and documentaries showing how bad some children are treated. But I was never really abused or neglected like *that*. So what you are saying really doesn't apply to me." But, not so fast. Denial is one of our primary, emotional defenses. Every one of us is in some way affected by early A/D realities. Do you remember what I said about perceived emotional abuse and neglect? Can you remember feeling fear, anger, or guilt as a child in relation to encounters with authority? I am not just talking about abuse. Neglect (intentional or unintentional) has even deeper and more profound effects.

She was sitting in my office saying something about not knowing what to talk about or why she was even there. She had come from a close and caring family, the second of three sisters, all of whom were loved and cared for by parents who had demonstrated their love, not just for their children, but also for each other.

I asked her to tell me her story and she did. She was right: there was no real abuse or neglect, no serious scars from her past, and currently she was in a great marriage with her childhood sweetheart. "So," she said, "why do I have these deep feelings of fear of abandonment?" After my further probing of her life story, she mentioned (almost as an afterthought) that off and on (during the first couple of years of her life) her mother had struggled with some health issues that would land her in the hospital for, sometimes, weeks at a time. When I asked who cared for her during that time, she said that a number of family members and friends took turns caring for her. Although it was nobody's fault, she was neglected during her early years of life, being deprived of the care she was born to expect from her mother. A good mother always has a much greater vested interest in her child than any friends or family who attempt to fill the void. How can we blame a mother for being sick? Interestingly enough, she had little memory of the other caretakers through the years. It was as if when her mother was away, her world went on hold.

Life: A Series of A/D Relationships

If you were to think back over your life story, there are probably many A/D transactional events that would come to mind, evoking feelings of fear, anxiety, shame, or anger (depending on how quickly your mind would allow them to surface). If not with parents, these transactional events would be with other authority figures such as teachers, aunts and uncles, older siblings, or any other of the numerous individuals who were in a position of power and control over you.

He was probably in his late forties (though he looked fifteen years older) as he sat in my office, attempting to deal with all the "bad hands" that life had dealt him. Unhappily married with two adult children (he was disconnected from both), he had come to a place, if the truth were known, of actually disliking them. And so he asked me, "How can you dislike your own children?" It became obvious that he was suffering from a severe depression that he had been trying to shake for years. He was an elementary school teacher. When I asked him if he liked his job, the answer was, "No. In fact, I really don't even like kids." In the next chapter, I am going to talk about Inner Healing and the power of the Holy Spirit to identify and heal the troubled and traumatic memories that have shaped our mental/emotional landscape. I mention that because, at this point in the story of the schoolteacher, I enlisted the help of the Holy Spirit to find out why he was in my office. He wasn't of a mindset to seek counseling, since his beliefs were dominated by a rigid fundamentalism that was suspicious of experiences with the Holy Spirit. Emotional pain, however, is a tremendous motivator.

After getting the schoolteacher's permission, I asked the Holy Spirit to bring to his mind any memory He would choose that would help us to understand what was going on in this man's soul. Since his belief system did include a belief in the Holy Spirit (although academic, not experiential) he closed his eyes and we waited. It wasn't long before he began to rub his face just below his left eye. I knew God was doing *something* because often the *body* remembers traumatic events *before* the picture actually comes into our minds. He shook his head and said, "I don't really know why this came into my head. I haven't thought about this for a long time." Then the story spilled out about how, when in early grade school, he had been on the playground at recess during a snowball fight. Someone had put a rock in one of the snowballs. It had struck him on the face, causing him to bleed. When he showed his injury to a teacher, instead of receiving sympathy, he was blamed and labeled a troublemaker. Shortly thereafter, he was hauled off to the principal's office. His feelings of shame and outrage knew no time. Although the memory was buried, it became a powerful force in shaping his filter. Could it be a coincidence that when he grew up, he became an elementary school teacher?

No Coincidence

Although I could not prove that there is a direct connection between the issues of his past and his career decisions as an adult, it is probably no coincidence. It was no coincidence either that there were now relational problems with his wife and kids. His rigid fundamentalism (that I mentioned earlier) was a continuation of what generations of his ancestors had handed down to their offspring in their beliefs and practices. When I asked him if he ever felt close to his parents, especially his father, he quickly responded in the negative. When little attachment is made in childhood with the significant "A's" in one's life, the ability to attach to *anyone* and experience any expected level of intimacy in adulthood becomes difficult. This would include not only a spouse, but also even one's own children. When we have A/D issues, they may get triggered no matter upon which side of the equation we find ourselves.

Remember our question at the beginning of the chapter: "What is the D's responsibility in relation to authority?" Think about it: if the message sent and accepted was that it was the dependent's responsibility for relationship, then how can the "D" even begin to get her/his head around Relational Rule Number One? Instead, events will be interpreted through a filter that is shaped and dominated by fear, anger, or shame. Attempts to deal with current, perceived threats will be irrational, counterproductive, and even destructive to current A/D relationships, especially the high-stakes relationships with spouses and children. Meanwhile, we remember our schoolteacher, whose distant and rigid relationship with wife and kids is born out of ancient beliefs, resulting in a disconnected isolation from those who are most important to him. Although I could not prove it, the childhood control issues (originating through the unhealthy responses of a teacher and a principal) led to an attempted resolution in adulthood. The attempt at resolution was to become a schoolteacher. This, however, became *the problem*. The loss of hope of anything changing left him depressed and resigned to his miserable life. The sadness was compounded by the fact that he was a talented, gifted, and frustrated writer whose closet was full of exquisite and publishable poetry and short stories.

Tenacious Encoded Beliefs

When beliefs about the way things are become encoded on our brains, they are very difficult to root out, even when they are causing tremendous emotional and/or physical pain. Many a therapist has said, "If you can change a person's beliefs, you can change his life." These beliefs include the relationship between authority and dependency, permission to feel and express emotion (either at *the drop of a hat* or not at all) and the expectancy of care from the individual who is in authority.

Perhaps the most tenacious belief to root out is the belief that *I am responsible* for relationship with authority. I have to initiate and determine the quality of relationship with anyone in authority over me. If I don't, then either bad things will happen or there won't be any of the longed-for relationships with the essential "A's" in my life. Once I accept this responsibility, however, the feelings of fear, anxiety, guilt and shame, or anger and rage can overwhelm me with anxiety or depression, as I attempt to survive or keep myself in check. It is rare that I ever even ask the question, "What is in it for me?"

Relational Rule # 2

Keeping in mind the truth of Relational Rule Number One, we move to Relational Rule Number Two: *Obedience is a Choice*. God set up this world with the intention of giving us freedom. We have the right to choose under whose or what authority we wish to come. I know this is not the case at birth. We do not choose our parents or families. But the good news is that we grow up and, in that process, gain the power and control over our own wills. While this is (in fact) true, it often doesn't feel that way because the systems into which we were born have a long history of violating Relational Rule Number One. I know that it is equally difficult to believe that the creator of the universe set up the world in such a way as to allow his creation to *choose* submission under His natural authority over us or not. But the simple truth of the matter is that He did. This *choosing* is called free will, and fathoming the depth of this reality is to understand who God is at the core of His being and the way His creation operates.

You Have A Choice

When we begin to talk about God' s Kingdom coming and His will being done on earth as it is in heaven (which we recite as part of *The Lord's Prayer)* consider this: *you have a choice.* Actually you have a number of choices about how to relate to the ultimate authority. You may choose to join the rebellion against God, led by the fallen archangel, Lucifer (also know as satan). This rebellion employs a multi-faceted approach, but mostly relies on lies, deceit, and promises of earthly power, riches, or simply the release from pain. There is also the vague, bogus guarantee that bad things won't happen now or in the future if you placate him (satan) through invitation and continued worship. Making this choice demands complete preoccupation and devotion of the soul to the particular religious system over which satan has gained control. All pagan religious systems fall into this category. The big lie: there are many roads that lead to God.

You may choose to believe that all of what we call earth and life happens by chance or is "random stuff" that is a result of a big bang and the survival of the fittest. Something came from nothing or, at least, from something else that we have yet to learn about. Only the unenlightened and primitive, superstitious mind could believe in a creator, God. I may not have accurately portrayed the secular, humanist, post-modern, enlightened and sophisticated worldview, but I am probably close.

It may be that you may choose to believe some conglomeration of various beliefs, including those mentioned above mixed with what we call Judeo-Christian. Others believe in a materialism that worships the self because, in their beliefs, *that is all there is* and, of course, we all know that *you only go around once in life.* The fact of the matter is that we are actually free to believe what we choose, remembering, of course, that there are consequences to what we choose.

Obedience & Choice

While I have attempted to give some sense of the power we have to choose, there may be a problem of perception with the word, "obedience." Obedience is one of those words so encrusted with all kinds of A/D "crud" that to pair it with the word "choice," seems like an oxymoron. The two words/concepts just don't seem to go together any more than an Ohio State fan wearing a Michigan hat on game day. So let me take some time to define (or perhaps redefine) the idea of *choosing* to submit to authority and its rules. Again I am not using the word rule, but rather rules. Rule also has negative vibes, especially when coupled with the word "over," as in "rule over." It seems to suggest the selfish use of authority for the benefit of the "A" and not the "D." Why, if we have a choice, would we choose to submit to a selfish tyrant? Choosing to do so would make us a little (if not, a lot*) crazy.*

Coach Young

But sometimes the person in authority *gets it right.* Over the course of my rocky and tumultuous career in sports (from the fifth grade through college) I had over thirty different coaches in four different sports. Some were better than others in their Authority/Dependency relationship between coach and player. Many coaches take on almost mythical proportions as god-like, father figures from Knute Rockney to Vince Lombardi to Sparky Anderson. There is no question in my mind that the one who stands head and shoulders above all the other coaches I ever had was Coach Young.

I had coaches who were more personable, more knowledgeable and less demanding about the game. I can remember many times literally crawling into the shower after a long, bone-numbing practice, unable to move for twenty minutes or more. There were times I was told in no uncertain terms in front of the whole team that I was not where I was supposed to be on the basketball floor, that I was not doing what I was supposed to be doing, and that he wondered where my brain was anyway. Although I was not a star player or one of his favorites (Coach Young didn't play favorites), I would choose to play for Coach Young anytime, anywhere. Coach Young, you see, took the time to establish a relationship with me. He initiated and shaped that relationship. There was never a question about accepting responsibility; he always did. And still, his rules were the toughest I ever encountered.

Coach Young, perhaps more than any other coach I ever met, absolutely hated to lose a game. He instilled this passion in all his players. When we did lose, we were taught to act with dignity, but never to accept losing. We rarely lost, although usually smaller and, in many ways, less talented than our opponents.

I remember once, on a long three-and-one-half hour bus ride home following a gut-wrenching loss to a conference rival, one of our marquee players was *acting up* with a fellow teammate at the back of the bus. After an initial warning that went unheeded, Coach Young walked to the back of the bus and informed the then stunned player to *clean out his locker* upon our return. That was it—star player or no star player. We all knew he was serious. The player cleaned out his locker. Just to put this event in perspective, this player (who was a phenomenal athlete) had been offered a full-ride scholarship to a Big Ten University in football, where he went on to become an all-conference player. The following week during practice, the Coach called the team together because the player had had a talk with coach and had something to say to us. As he stood before us, he drew a deep breath and then apologized to the team for his behavior. After doing so, he was allowed to put his "stuff" back in his locker. Both he and the team were better for the event and I imagine, forty years later, every member of that team remembers the lesson of responsibility that the coach taught us that week.

Why so much talk about sports? Sports, in many ways, can be a microcosm of life. In the former case, it tells a story about obedience, relationship and choices. We don't necessarily choose to submit to the rules of an authority because the rules are easy; often, the rules are difficult and challenging. But if the one administering the rules is fair and has taken the time to establish relationship, we come to realize that this authority *is* acting in our best interest; and not merely ours alone, but (often) the collective, best interest of our fellow travelers on the way. Whether we consider our role on a team, in a class, in the workplace, at church, in a family, as a citizen, or as a child of God (all of which involve Authority/Dependency relationships), remember this: we were all created with a free will, allowing us the ability to choose whether or not to come into an A/D relationship with our creator and obey the rules of His kingdom.

But I Didn't Have A Choice

I know what you're thinking: there are many circumstances under which we don't have a choice, such as who our parents are or the natural realities of climate and gravity. That is true, to the extent that we don't *spit into the wind* or stand under a tree during a thunderstorm. We do not remain children, however; we grow up (at least, that is the plan). Neither do we remain perpetual students; some of us grow up to be teachers.

I will never forget my first day in the first grade. His name was Chester (not actually his real name), and he was not happy to be in school. He had no trouble showing it. When Mrs. Dreadful (not her real name) began to chase Chester around the room, my normally laid-back mind went on alert. It wasn't fair really. She was bigger and faster. She quickly caught him and then proceeded to pull out "ole hickory." She gave his behind a good paddlin' in front of the whole class (this was in the days when spanking was not only permissible, but encouraged). You can draw your own conclusions as to whether or not that was a good thing. I decided then and there, I wasn't going to like school and, for the next sixteen years, I never did. Then (strangely enough) in grad school when I began studying a subject I actually enjoyed, I found myself actually "liking school." Later, when asked to teach at the undergraduate level, I found myself actually enjoying teaching. It is why I tell people, "I never liked school until I got to be the teacher."

Obedience & Defense Mechanisms

As children, so much of what *passes* as obedience is actually a defense mechanism or survival style in response to the abuse or the neglect of authority. The focus becomes the rules, especially with the legalistic crowd. What gets lost in the mess and confusion of the accusations is relationship. After all, how many of us have actually come under the authority of someone who we truly believe will act in our best interest?

James didn't. For just over ten years, he had been pursuing his education and training as a doctor, first as an undergrad, later in med school, and finally as a resident in his "chosen" field of interest. So why was he now sitting in my office in a "shut down" state of virtual emotional and physical paralysis? Slowly the story of his life over the last ten years spilled out. "My life has been a virtual hell," he shared. "I never really wanted to be a doctor." So why would someone spend ten years doing just that—denying one's own interests, in order to devote hours to study and everything else connected with being a doctor? The answer was simple. "It is what I thought my father wanted me to be." Ever the obedient son, (ten years later) James was a doctor. But it was not his choice. So why do it? In this case, obedience was not a choice; instead, it was an attempt on the part of a son to please his dad. Pleasing is a defense mechanism. In this case, it was a profound belief that (as a son) he was responsible for relationship. He believed that if he didn't become a doctor, he would never receive the affirmation and care he so desperately desired from his father. Who among us doesn't desire the same thing?

Righteousness

To add to the confusion, let me suggest a concept that we have been taught from the time we entered Sunday school. It is called "righteousness," and is, basically, the moral injunction to think and act rightly. I challenge you right now to define for yourself the word righteousness, and discover if you do not feel the *demand* implied in that definition. I am not suggesting that to live righteously is not demanding; it is. But void of relationship and the purpose given in that relationship by authority, demand *becomes demanding,* feels controlling, and causes one to believe that he/she is responsible for the relationship, especially with God Himself.

Jesus Loves Me This I Know?

For so many of us, there is not a place (even in our minds) that can conceive of this kind of freedom in relationship with authority, let alone begin to believe that it could happen with God Himself. Jesus loves me; this I know, for the Bible tells me so. Okay. That *is* what it says; but that has not been my experience with any authority. Jesus may love me, but probably much like my mother or father does. That love is full of guilt, shame, and confusion (and that is just for starters). The result is that we learn, at a very early age, to lock our real selves away somewhere. This is the effect of the violation of Relational Rule Number One: the locked up, boarded up, walled up, iron doors of the guarded soul. It doesn't really matter if (as a result) we become pleaser/placaters or rebellious agnostics.

Experience has taught us to be and to live this way. Only experience can change our beliefs. In the next chapter, I'll talk about an experiential relationship with our creator (who can and does tell us the truth about our lives and His relationship with us). Could Relational Rule Number Two actually be true? Is it really our choice? As Lucy asks Mr. Tumnus in *The Lion, the Witch, and the Wardrobe*, "Is Aslan safe?" Can He really restore what the locust has eaten? Can His kingdom coming and His will being done on earth as it is in heaven be a good thing? Or is He (as the ultimate authority) merely placing the responsibility for relationship on us, the "D's?"

Obedience = Relationship

I am not sure I know what you're thinking, but perhaps I have inadvertently succeeded in confusing you in my attempt to explain the word, *obedience,* by equating it with relationship. In the end, the two words cannot be separated, for obedience cannot be rightly defined without understanding the connection to relationship. In this relationship, the one being obeyed has made it clear that your best interest is not only paramount but is, in fact, the goal of the relationship and has been from the beginning.

Now About Relationship's Rules

As if obedience and choice weren't already elusive enough to understand, let's throw in responsibility. Remember in Relational Rule Number One that responsibility comes with being in authority. We have spent some time trying to make that clear, setting obedience and choice in their rightful place in relationship. Perhaps now we can begin to talk about that for which the "D" is responsible. But let's make something clear from the start: *being responsible for* relationship and *having responsibilities in* a relationship are *not* the same thing. What do I mean by that? The point is simply that all relationships have rules that govern them, and once we make the choice to be in relationship, we accept those rules. For example, if I choose to live in Buffalo, N.Y., I need to keep my boots and winter coat in a closet somewhere. There are *rules* for living in Buffalo. I may want to break the rules and choose to wear shorts and a T-shirt all year, but . . . I think you "get the picture." Once I choose to live in Buffalo, it becomes my responsibility to dress in warm clothes when the weather demands. When I chose to play for Coach Young, I expected a rigorous training schedule. It was my responsibility to get in shape. If I didn't work hard in practice, I could expect the admonitions that would invariably come. "D's" do have responsibilities; but if those responsibilities are forced upon us against our wills, we soon learn about *the stuff* of which "crazy" is made. The point is that *relationship does not equal rules* and *rules do not equal relationship.*

Survival Can Look Crazy

When responsibility for my own emotional and physical survival is forced upon me, of course, I do what I *need to do* to survive. Sometimes that can look a little crazy to other people. Sometimes it can be offensive to other people. Sometimes it becomes self-destructive; but it is the way life is. I necessarily have to take care of myself.

What if I desire to be in relationship with a particular "A," like a parent or a spouse, and realize that this person either doesn't want to be in relationship with me or is oblivious or somehow incapable? Not long ago, I spent some time in a part of the old Soviet Union, teaching a seminar for a church. This is one place in the world where, for centuries, those in positions of authority have *not* been acting in the people's best interest. Most recently (under the Politburo) the government set out to convince the people that they were responsible to the state. And, frankly, they did a good job of literally dividing and conquering the family structure, telling the people that their children belonged to the state and that they were no longer needed as parents. As it turned out, the State was a horrendously neglectful (and an often abusive) surrogate parent.

Following the seminar, I was asked to speak at the Sunday morning church service. I felt it applicable to talk about fathers and their children. At the end of the service, I told the congregation that I (along with the other men who had accompanied me) were going to approach each father and pray a father's blessing over them. This was, of course, optional and they did not have to submit to our blessing them. There were some who quietly motioned that they did not wish to receive a blessing. Their wishes were respected and no judgments were made. A few days later (in conversation with one of the interpreters) I learned that she was at the back of the church when we moved into the congregation to bless the men. She said that there were a number of men who were literally *running* out of the church. A blessing seems like a good thing. Right? If so, why (for these men) was it something to run from? The pastor of the church for the past thirteen years suggested that responsibility was not something easily embraced. This is true not just in the old Soviet Union but also most everywhere in the world.

Honor Your Father & Mother

Perhaps there is no man (or anyone else in a position of authority) who really understands responsibility and readily accepts it. If this is the case, what do *we* do if we are dependent on them, short of becoming *crazy?* Many times I have been asked the question, "How do I honor parents who are *not honorable?*" "How do I survive if I have to live in the chicken coop *with the fox?*

At the risk of beating (as they say) *a dead horse,* the core issue is the concept of choice. (By the way, they say you can't move a dead horse; but this is actually not true. You *can move* a dead horse, but it takes a considerable amount of strength and energy. The dead horse, of course, will remain in the same place you left it. It will also begin to stink. Do you know what I mean?) But enough about dead horses and on to an understanding of living with foxes and honoring the dishonorable.

What To Do About Bad Authority

We often find ourselves in a relationship under the authority of someone who is not acting in our best interest (and that may be putting it mildly). Those in positions of authority threaten the emotional survival of those dependent upon and vulnerable to their power and control. Foxes in the chicken coop can be parents, spouses, teachers, bosses, priests or anyone (or anything) holding the position of authority over us. When this is the case, the natural response is to engage an emotional defense. This often happens with no conscious knowledge of what we are doing. Remember that when we engage these emotional defenses, they operate based upon the belief that we (the " D's") are responsible for relationship. Explaining how to relate to foxes in a healthy way becomes very tricky.

Let's suppose that I am a *pleaser*. It is my emotional defense against abuse and neglect. It is my way of getting some of the care I expect (or at least preventing some of the neglect or abuse). When I choose to please (out of that place in my soul) I really feel I have no choice. If I don't please, then bad things are going to happen. If I don't please, then it is made clear to me that the reason bad things did happen is my fault; I am responsible. This, of course, is truly a violation of Relational Rule Number One. But who is *policing* the foxes or blowing the whistle and calling a foul? That's right. It doesn't usually happen. Consequently, we come to believe that is *just the way of it.* Our survival style kicks in and we continue to please.

Then, at some point, it becomes obvious to us that pleasing isn't really working either. Although we continue to please, we still get abused and neglected. Finally we decide that we are not going to be a pleaser any more. Bad things continue to happen, however, and are sometimes worse than before. We end up being confused and angry or physically sick, anxious and depressed. We have lost all hope of obtaining that *longed-for life,* asking, "Where is God in all of this? The reality of life is that there are real foxes out there whose lives seem dependent upon malicious control of others vulnerable to their power through abuse and neglect. There are others who are simply ignorant of or oblivious to their own destructiveness. But the results are the same: bad things happen to the "D's" of this world.

So How Do We Survive?

The question then becomes: How do we survive them? If we don't first give ourselves permission to believe and understand the truth of Relational Rule Number One (that they hold responsibility for acting in our best interest) and Relational Rule Number Two (that we may *choose* to obey them), then we won't gain any measure of health or control of our lives (especially while living in the chicken coop). Let's return to our "pleaser." There is nothing wrong with wanting to please someone in authority (even though they are abusing the privilege and don't deserve the courtesy). We may still choose to please them. Perhaps this sounds like doubletalk. The keyword here is "choose." When we choose, *we* are in control. There is a difference between employing a pleasing, defense mechanism and consciously deciding to please someone. Once that decision is made, we are consciously ready to accept the consequences and can adjust to them accordingly.

Strategy vs. Unconscious Defense Mechanism

Now our action becomes a strategy versus an unconscious defense. When we see that the strategy is not working, we may choose another. It may have seemed to any first century observer that that old fox, Herod, the Roman ruler, Pilot, and the corrupt, Jewish Sanhedrin had taken Jesus' life from him. Jesus made it clear that this was not the case. He said He was giving His life out of His own power to choose. When we believe we are acting out of our own choice, we feel in control, even if bad things are happening.

Recently I was waiting in a Kinko's store for the next available person to help me. I was standing next to the rack of books for sale. One book, in particular, caught my eye. It was called, *Get Anyone to do Anything* by David J. Lieberman. I thought, "Wouldn't that be nice?" So I bought the book. In the book were several strategies to use in various situations to do just that: get others to do what you want. The concept is actually very realistic. As we learn some basic concepts about human motivation, it becomes clear that (if we choose) we can have more control over our lives. There are strategies we can learn and employ to stay in control and in a safer place.

Choice & Control

In my reading of history (particularly those who survived great oppression, violence, or tragedy), the power to choose played a key role. When prisoners, for example, who have been stripped of all that is human, are thrown into dark dungeons and lose their sense of control, they usually die. When they somehow are able to exert some measure of control over their environment through some sort of routine (as in the marking of days) or maintaining control of their own minds (through the recitation of something from memory) they are able against all odds to survive.

Of course, in a prison, there is no question that there will be violations of relationships and that bad things are going to happen. But in the case of relationships with parents or bosses, the violations are not *black and white,* but fade into *gray.* We are left confused and defensive. It is very often difficult to see our parents for who they were or are. Not all parental abuse and neglect is selfish or intentional. Parents can be victims as well. But to minimize their abusive and/or neglectful behavior toward us (for any reason) muddies the waters and serves only to reinforce the employment of emotional survival styles. Introspection is essential. We know when we feel in control or when we do not, when we are minimizing or excusing, or when we are just emotionally surviving.

Honoring Dishonorable Parents

Honoring dishonorable parents must include an honest, personal appraisal of who they are, what they have done, and the effects their actions have had on us before we can choose how to respond. It is difficult to choose the control of an emotion when a defense kicks in so quickly that conscious choice never enters the picture. The same is true of surviving all abuse and neglect of authority. When we are left in a bad situation, if we can think things through to the point of choosing, we will find ourselves in control. Remember: it is all about control. If we have control (by choice) we can stay emotionally and, very often, physically safe, even when forced to exist in the chicken coop with the fox. In we are unable to do this, we may find ourselves in a bad place, feeling trapped. This can really make us feel *crazy*, the kind of crazy that causes us to question if we are losing our minds. What we have lost is control of our ability to, first, be in touch with our survival emotion and then to make conscious decisions for ourselves.

The Question of Control

We need to be aware of one other thing about being in control, even if we are in a dependent position. This particular truth I learned from my kids. Whoever is asking the questions is usually the person who is in control. Let me ask you, "What happens when you tell your kids it is time for bed?" In my house, it triggers a barrage of questions intended to keep the A/D power struggle in balance (because they don't want to go to bed right now). "Can I just stay up ten more minutes or finish watching this program?" Can I have a drink of water or a peanut butter and jelly sandwich? Will you read me a story? I am guessing you can add a few hundred questions of your own.

Avoiding Defensiveness

When dealing with foxes, there are a couple of enemies to your survival that are to be avoided like the plague. The first is *defensiveness*, and not just in A/D relationships. This is true for all relationships. Avoiding defensiveness, by virtue of definition, puts you in control. Whoever put you on the defensive is in control and, while defensiveness is intended to defend us against accusations or emotional pain (because if we don't defend ourselves, who will?), in most cases, defensiveness is counterproductive. In the end, it tends to make matters worse. Instead of exerting control and thus reducing emotional pain, we find ourselves getting hurt anyway. It is often better to say nothing at all. But it is very tough in high-stakes relationships (especially with spouses) to avoid these *emotional hijacks*. It feels like if we don't say something or set the record straight, the current issue with which we are dealing will never get resolved. "Resolved" is another of those vague concepts for which everyone thinks he/she knows the definition, when resolution really means quite different things to different people.

Spontaneity May Be Your Enemy

The second enemy, when dealing with foxes, is *spontaneity*. When living in or going to the chicken coop, you must have a plan and you must follow the plan. This is because, to a certain extent, being with foxes (especially in the chicken coop) is like being at war. This can, of course, be very confusing. Remember the longings we carry from unmet expectations? The thinking goes something like this: if I spend time with the people from whom I desire care (even if they are not safe) it will give them the opportunity to give me that care; if I distance myself from them emotionally or physically, then I will never get my longings resolved. When the result is continued abuse or neglect, often there are not enough medications to keep us functioning. There are not enough of (what I call) the self-medicated attempts (such as food, chemicals, sex, pornography, nicotine, caffeine, and extra jobs) either to *minimize the pain* or *to keep the pain away*.

The "Holiday Talk"

Usually in November, I have the *"Holiday Talk"* with my clients. Holidays can be the worst time of year for those who come from dysfunctional families. Weddings, funerals, or any type of family gathering (where one's presence is *expected*) also fit into this category. The difficulty arises because the pilgrimage to the coop with the fox or awaiting the fox's pilgrimage to you is a time of expected and longed-for connection, especially at Thanksgiving and Christmas. It is supposed to look something like a Walton's or a Hallmark holiday, where (although stressful things may happen and the outcome is uncertain) the family values triumph in the end. The problem with dysfunctional families is that while stressful things happen, nothing gets resolved and the trip back home is sullen and gray with feelings of hopelessness.

Got To Have A Plan

As in war, you need a strategy to deal with those who can hurt you, especially in high-stakes, family relationships. Spontaneous happenings usually turn into disasters, even though you have the best intentions. Our heart is really just to hang out with those essential others, hoping we will *happen onto* a connecting moment. But when the spontaneous moments happen, they are usually full of conflicting agendas and expectations.

Last Thanksgiving, I was spending the holiday with my children and grandchildren, having an awesome time. The turkey was in the oven; the pumpkin pies and all the rest of the wonderful, family, traditional dishes we enjoy were awaiting us. Then, it happened. We needed something from the grocery store. So I volunteered for the job and, momentarily, forgot my own counsel to avoid spontaneity. I asked if one of the grandkids could accompany me. I was thinking that I would go to the store and perhaps, at the same time, spend some quality time with one of my grandkids. The problem was that eight grandkids were present (now nine) and four of them wanted to go with me. Okay, I thought. I can take four. Besides, I don't want to disappoint any of them (quality time and all). The next problem was transportation and car seats; we couldn't put the little ones in the front seat with the air bags. Next, of course, we had to find their shoes, and three of them had to go to the bathroom. My number-five grandchild wasn't wearing pink and would not be caught dead outside the house, if not in pink. Pretty soon the tears began to flow and I remembered my own advice. I had to go to the store alone, realizing that I would have already been back by now if I had gone on my own, alone.

I know what you're thinking. It all sounds like a lot of hard work. Why can't we just learn to treat each other with care and respect? Why do relationships (especially what you call *high-stakes* relationships with parents and spouses) have to be so difficult and full of potential, relational landmines? My only answer is to say something about *the heart of man* and that *caldron* of past events, emotions, beliefs, and coping strategies.

Because we were created as relational beings, it would seem that relationships should occur naturally. Am I right? But (you may have noticed) relationships of quality and connectedness that satisfy the deep longings in our souls are few and far between. With centuries of relational violations of Relational Rule Number One and no sense of any real choices, Relational Rule Number Two seems like a pipe dream. Where and how do we begin to fix all of this? I suggest that we start at the beginning. *In the beginning, God . . .*

CHAPTER SEVEN

Redemption, Restoration & Healing

Redemption, Restoration, and Healing. These are awesome concepts, if they are indeed true. The problem is that practically none of us actually believe that anything like redemption, restoration and healing really occurs this side of paradise. How many of us believe the old adage that "life is hard and then you die" or "nothing ever really changes; people are who they are?" There are many sayings that allude to our frustration and resignation to the difficulties and so-called realities of our lives. "You have to get over it; it's time to move on. Why not deal with it and put it in your past?"

Dealing with these concepts, counselors often use different approaches. We listen with empathy and compassion, applying our therapeutic models as best we can. We offer the hope of less pain and better functioning. We go to dark places with our clients, offering support and comfort. It is hard work. For some, there is a lessening of pain and an increase of functioning; but restoration seems like a *stretch.*

The Medicinal Approach

Other times, we entertain the possibility that with the right medications, we may be able to address the *bad chemistry* going on in the brain. Our goal is to get the serotonins and dopamines balanced and reuptaking (or not reuptaking) correctly. Since there is such a large, genetic component anyway, to a certain extent it seems there are some aspects over which we have little control; consequently, we have to go with the *meds.* I certainly have seen the positive effects of a rightly tailored treatment plan employing meds. Many people feel better, cope better, and relate better when on medication. The technology in psychotropic medications has increased tremendously in recent years. Although it is often difficult to get over the stigma of weakness attached to taking medication, the fact of the matter is that meds are a common part of millions of individuals' daily regimen. Medicinal support for our emotional well-being is not, however, what we would refer to as *healing*.

There was a resignation in his voice that *spoke volumes* to me. His marriage of twenty-two years was (for all practical purposes) over. His wife had left him and was living with another man. The pain of that reality was almost too much for him to bear; and yet, a part of him must have known this would happen. Three children in their early and mid-teens, now looked to him to learn what would happen next. He was struggling with his own pain, trying desperately to support them in theirs. There had been many signs of her unfaithfulness over the years that he had chosen to ignore. But her inability to connect or bond with her children was incomprehensible to him. "We tried to tell you dad," the kids told him, "but you were just in some kind of denial." As he sat in my office, head in his hands, shaking it in disbelief, he finally said what many say, "I prayed and prayed for God to change her, and I really believed He would."

But God hadn't changed her, and the family had suffered decades of neglect and abuse. The years of suffering seemed to everyone like a wasteland of human survival. How could those years ever be redeemed? How could God ever restore what the locust had eaten?

Relational Rule Includes God

There are many who ask, "Aren't we actually witnessing the problem of sin, the heart of man, and the correct application of the scriptural principles of *repentance, forgiveness, or deliverance?*" Probably all of the above are true and more. Yet so many of our solutions are based upon beliefs that actually *stand in the way* of any true redemption, restoration, or healing. Simply put, our solutions are based upon (more or less) total violations of Relational Rule Number One because they assume that one holds the responsibility for one's own healing. Could there possibly be another way to think and believe? Do you remember Relational Rule Number One? In essence, whoever is in the position of authority initiates and shapes the quality of relationship and is responsible for it. That includes God. Redemption, restoration and healing are *His initiatives* poured out on us (His children), not because we are correctly applying scripture to our lives, but because He chooses to pour out a *mercy* that is beyond human understanding.

She was the paragon of all that is desired or held in esteem by peers and generations above and below her. She could have stepped out of a *Vogue* magazine or made the cover of *Good Housekeeping*. She was beautiful, in her mid-thirties, and successfully married to an established professional, with one gifted and talented child, a boy. She was engaging and approachable, having arrived in her white BMW SUV. In short, she was perfect. If so, why was she sitting in my office? To look at her, how would anyone ever suspect that on the inside, her soul was a scarred and desolate landscape, haunted by past demons and experiences of the deepest neglect and abuse? I was her fifth counselor.

Emotional Pain Not Always Obvious

You see, with some of us, it is obvious that we have problems, from the way we look to the way we talk or interact with the world around us. With others, their *issues* are not as obvious. So what do I tell the "thirty-something" mother in my office? "Keep doing what you're doing; it seems to be working. You have the perfect life, the perfect husband, the perfect child, the perfect beliefs, no big sins, and no obvious issues." Some say that *living well is the best revenge*. Given her past, she was living very well. Nonetheless, she was in tremendous pain, and the current status of her life could not convince her that *this is as good as it gets*. She needed healing; and only God can heal. In varying degrees, most of us need redemption, restoration and healing. And just like our young mother, we probably look *just fine*. Not surprisingly, if we were asked the question, "How are you?," our answer would be the same, "Just fine."

Redemption, Restoration & Healing = One Word

Let me pause a minute and give you some definitions. If you were to read the definitions of the words, *redemption* or *restoration,* in the dictionary, you would be given merely the *surface (or first layer)* of a great depth existing in the redemption, restoration, and healing of which I am talking. Rather than defining them separately, I want to *scrunch* them all together as if they were actually one word. I know what you're thinking. Is he allowed to do that? I admit that this is probably taking some liberty and, yes, it is true that I slept through English grammar class. Nevertheless, when we *jerry winkle* the three words together, what does the result look like? Actually, it is yet another definition of God. It is only God who can make all things new this side of eternity; making all things new takes some supernatural redemption, restoration, and healing.

Oblivious Arrogance

I had never seen a person who was so full of arrogance and pride yesterday, but a blubbering, broken, hulk of a man today as the man before me. He knew he had to change, but really didn't have a clue how. His wife of eighteen years had packed up and left, taking their two children to her parents. I didn't disagree with her decision. They had been in counseling for almost nine months, getting nowhere because he didn't believe they really had any problems. If anyone needed counseling, he believed it was she. One time he confided in me that he felt she had *serious issues from her past.* Perhaps what was needed was for her to work on those issues (with me, but without him). Although his past was no *walk in the park,* he felt that he had dealt with his issues and had *gotten over them.*

The wife set up an appointment with me (alone) sobbing, heaving, and repeating over and over again how she had tried (at first, for the children; later, because of the economics involved; and finally, because she was *"just plain scared of going to hell."*) "Would God send me to hell for leaving a man who has emotionally and (once) physically abused me? Would He punish me even though I have been treated as if I am an object ever since our honeymoon? This is a man who treats our children like they are slaves in their own home. I wish he would just have an affair. Then I would have permission from the church to divorce him." She saw the situation as hopeless, and I had difficulty disagreeing with her. The oblivious arrogance in this man was *off the charts.* Eight months of counsel had accomplished nothing. I believed the marriage had less than a ten-percent chance of lasting for the year.

Her leaving, however, had somehow dented his wall of pride, touching something in him that hadn't been vulnerable to touch perhaps since he was in diapers. If you knew him, you wouldn't believe that could ever happen. I think he was shocked at his own pain. "Let's give it a few weeks,'" I told him somewhat cavalierly. "The pain will subside and then you can decide what you want to do about your marriage." He wanted to schedule another appointment later that week, but I said, "No. Let's wait a couple of weeks." I really didn't expect to hear from him again.

Climbing the Mountain

Two weeks later he was back, with eyes sunken, face unshaved, looking like a rumpled mess and asking if I could save his marriage. I said, "No. I can't. But with *God's redeeming, restoring, healing love*, there is a chance to save it." When I later saw his wife, I suggested that she at least consult a lawyer, not knowing what he, her husband, might be capable of doing. Over the next few months, this man laid down his pride and, probably for the first time in his life, listened. He began to do the work—*climb the mountain*, as I call it. He began to accept the responsibility for his life and to understand that his beautiful wife and children were gifts from a loving God. He began to understand that he (as the husband and father) was responsible for relationship with them. Frankly, I have never seen a man work harder or grow up faster. His wife was naturally suspicious. She had begun to put her life in order and was enjoying the safety of *not living* under the same roof with him.

Nearly ten months later, I was beginning to see a different man. Softer, humbler, less angry and controlling, this husband continued to grow in his desire for another chance. His wife, on the other hand, had *moved on* with her life, and was somewhat surprised that the children seemed to enjoy their visits with their dad. One day, as I asked her about the separation and impending divorce, she said that she was saving her money in order to be able to afford a lawyer. When I suggested that I had seen some changes in her estranged husband, she became angry and threatened to discontinue counseling with me. She would find someone who could support *her*. I agreed that that was always her choice, but asked her just one question, "Do you believe in redemption, restoration, and healing?" She said she did in the abstract. But to believe that someone like her husband could change was beyond hope or possibility. "I lived with him for eighteen years; not you. You don't know him like I do."

It was the children who ended up pushing the issue. They were growing up and needing their dad (who, by the way, was actually becoming a "dad"). She waited until after the holidays for the trial homecoming, insisting on separate bedrooms and checking accounts, and making it clear that, at the first sign of the "old person," he was *out of there.* I told him that he had this *one chance* and that *many never get one.* He accepted the opportunity as one from God.

It Just Seems Miraculous

Things weren't perfect; he digressed occasionally into his controlling anger, but recovered quickly, making sincere amends. The *realness* of this new man became evident to everyone (especially his wife and severest critic). Ten months later, they celebrated their twentieth anniversary, more in love, more committed, and more functional than either could have imagined possible. *He* will tell you that it was an act of God; she would agree. I saw it for myself: the redeeming, restoring, healing power of the God of the universe who desired nothing more than to join the two together as one. They became deeply involved in the work of their church and community, not because that was something they were supposed to do, but because they so chose. No one (who knew them before) would call it anything but "a miracle." Healing, restoration and redemption are just that miraculous. But God doesn't see it that way. His desire from the beginning was for relationship and blessing. Free will and the heart of man, however, chose otherwise. I don't think this couple's miracle took God, by any means, by surprise. Redemption, restoration and healing were planned from the beginning.

Relationship & Blessing Intended From the Beginning

Relationships and blessings with and from God sound like wonderful concepts in the abstract. Imagine, the creator of the universe actually wanting to connect with me. I know what you're thinking. I tried that; it didn't work. Haven't we all, at some point in our lives, tried that? We asked God for something and then waited, only to be disappointed that either it didn't come or it never happened. Do we really *buy* all the *religious junk* we are taught by church people? What if those church people are our parents? We have to make some decisions about God at this point. For remember, we believe what we *experience.*

Too Late For Him

Why he ended up next to *me* while waiting for the maintenance to be completed on our cars, only God knows. I had so much work that I was going to complete; I was going to use my time waiting at the repair shop wisely. On my computer screen was a picture of my family and *that* started the conversation. He was thirty something, unmarried, and profoundly unhappy; nevertheless, he was curious about a family that might truly care about one another. Obviously, I cared enough about the people on my computer screen to put them there, knowing that I might see them every time I turned it on.

As a result of overhearing a cell phone conversation, he asked what I did for a living. When I told him that I was a counselor, he assumed from that piece of information and the picture on my screen that I must be happily married—something he revealed he wanted for himself. Although not perfect, I agreed I was happy in my marriage and suggested this was a possibility for him. "Oh, no," he said, "it is too late for me." When I suggested it is never too late for God, he said that he didn't believe in God. He had been raised and taught all that "God junk" and had actually *tested Him* those many years ago in the fourth grade: "If you are real, God, then will you . . . ?" He never told me what, in fact, the request was; only that his request *wasn't* answered. Further, he went on to ask if I was aware of all the injustices in the world. He wondered why, if God is all-powerful, He doesn't *do something* about them. He had drawn the only logical conclusion: there is no God.

He said he was an atheist, but I knew from his voice that that was not what he *wanted* to be. He wanted God to do something about whatever happened in elementary school, to supernaturally come down from heaven and change the course of his life. But that hadn't happened and that fact, for him, had determined the course of his life. Bad things do happen in this life. The battle is over and satan has won when those *bad things* are enough to suggest that *there is no God* or, if there is a God that He isn't very interested in what happens to me. Satan claims that God either doesn't exist or (if He does) that He is powerless. Even when satan concedes that He (God) may indeed have power, he argues that God doesn't care enough to use that power to help us with our *little problems.* I don't know what happened to my new friend in the fourth grade or why

God hadn't answered his prayer as he had hoped. I am certain that God had His reasons.

Playing God

I was reluctant to see the movie, "Bruce Almighty," a story about a human being (portrayed by Jim Carey, in this case) who was given the opportunity to be God for one day. But trusted friends reported that it was "pretty good" and not really sacrilegious, as I had supposed, so I decided to go. In it, there is an interesting scene where Bruce (the Jim Carey character) is in his apartment with his girlfriend. He has the idea to use his Godly powers to impress her. He goes to the balcony, reaches up, and draws the full moon closer to the earth. She *is* impressed, but (as Bruce finds out the next day) the people of Southeast Asia were *not so impressed* with the giant tides that swept over their coastal lands. So much for playing God!

We can be grateful that *God does not play God;* but sometimes, we wonder if He is even paying attention. We deal with many different foxes everywhere in this chicken coop called earth, wreaking havoc in our lives—from war and terrorism to domestic abuse; from deadly diseases to freak accidents and natural disasters that seem to come with increasing frequency.

The Cross & Relational Rule # 1

I know what you are thinking. I live in this world, too, and have both heard and experienced the stories. What I am about to suggest may startle you: the God of the universe *invented* Relational Rule Number One. He is the one who initiates relationship; he is the one who shapes relationship. He is the one who not only accepts responsibility for relationship, but also accepts all the blame and all the consequences for all the bad things that have ever happened or ever will. What do you think *the cross* was all about? Seriously, what do you think and believe about the axis of history, namely Jesus' life, death, and resurrection? I am telling you that it was for our redemption, restoration and healing.

God's Original Intent

In the book of Genesis, it tells us that the first man (Adam) walked with God in the garden, a place called paradise. I again suggest that

God's original intent for us was to be in relationship with Him and to bless us with all of His creation. We don't know how long Adam and Eve walked with God in the garden. Although it only takes a few minutes to read the first three chapters of Genesis, the actual time God spent in direct relationship with our first ancestors may have been as long as what we know to be thousands of years. While I am not going to take the time to talk about *how* satan ended up in that garden, he most certainly did. After deceiving first Eve and then Adam, he convinced them to join his rebellion against God that resulted in paradise lost. What was also lost in the process was the *quality* of relationship that Adam and Eve had experienced with their creator. Our first ancestors had a relationship with God that was physical, but more importantly spiritual. Although expelled from the garden we (sons and daughters of Adam, as C.S. Lewis calls us) were not totally abandoned, although there were now both physical and spiritual barriers between our Creator and us. The relationship became strained and difficult. Our fleshly, emotional souls rose to dominate and facilitate our survival, while our spirits set out to placate and please the serpent that had deceived us.

Never Abandoned

But God never lost His desire for relationship with us. Jesus Himself, through whom this world came into being, was coming to redeem and restore this relationship, healing what both man and satan had attempted to destroy. While we look forward to Jesus' second coming, we don't want to miss the point of His first coming. We find the account of His life on earth in the Gospels and the Acts of the Apostles. At the moment of Jesus' death on the cross, the barriers were removed. The curtain shielding the Holy of Holies, the very symbol of divine disassociation with His creation, was torn apart from top to bottom. God Himself removed the barriers. God was, in fact, in Christ reconciling the world, and especially us Sons and Daughters of Adam and Eve, to Himself.

Restoration Of Experiential Relationship

Then He sent the Holy Spirit through the most awesome display of His original intent for relationship and blessing seen since we walked with Him in the garden. The Holy Spirit is to accompany us on the journey until we are restored once again to paradise. He tells us that *if* we seek Him, we *will* find Him (if we seek Him with our whole heart). Seeking Him with our whole heart is not a command or a demand (as if you are damned if you don't); but rather, a precious opportunity to once again walk and talk with the creator of the universe.

While I love and study the Holy Scriptures given for my teaching, grounding and edification, I thank God that He doesn't expect me to just read and believe. God's plan is not: Father, Son and Holy Scripture; but Father, Son and Holy Spirit. The Holy Spirit is given for me to experience the power and the presence of a God who loves me and desires only my best interest. The experiential can be very subjective. God, however, (respecting our sovereign, free will) doesn't design our experiences as *one size fits all*. Because we are all so different and individual, God connects with each of us in a personal, *special* way. While that may seem unscientific and proves to often be *messy*, ultimately this is God's way of communicating with us individually. When He interacts with us, we *know* God has reached out to us, simply because it is so *unique* to our own experiences and beliefs.

A Religious Skeptic

I happen to be a religious skeptic, born out of fifty plus years in the church. While I loved the stories of the miraculous works of God in people's lives that I heard over the years, life (in my experience) was much the same outside the church as in. People were no more loving or less controlling in the church than outside the church. In fact, it often seemed to me that the church was a gathering place for sinners and hypocrites, where they might forget their state of being redeemed and engage in sinful and hypocritical activities not available to them in the world. I was coming to this conclusion even as people spoke about "this miraculous act" or "that word" that God spoke. I took it all with a grain of rice, or salt or whatever. God was always getting ready to do a *new thing* or a *new work* (always dependent, of course, on me for faith, sacrifice, or some other spiritual thing I couldn't quite understand). He had a plan for my life, the finding of which was somewhat akin to the quest for the Holy Grail or finding the Lost Ark of the Covenant. Please forgive my sarcasm, but it is important that you understand the depth of my skepticism.

Experiences of God and with God were shared, but the emphasis was on orthodoxy and right beliefs. If a person didn't have the *right* beliefs, perhaps one should not spend too much time with him/her. But, I wanted more. I had this sneaking suspicion that much of what went on in the church and passed as right beliefs were more man's ideas than the real God's ideas. The right beliefs, however, were " to seek not, and to forbid not" *the experiential stuff.* Besides, those who really sought after *experiences* were merely showing their lack of faith in so doing. "Blessed are those who have not seen (i.e. experienced) but have believed." I got the impression that the *just believe it approach* was the most spiritual. Interestingly enough, this is very similar to many people's relationship with their earthly fathers—relationships that are mostly academic and based on words, not true connections that are based on real experiences.

God Made Us This Way

When I read for myself about Jesus in the Gospels, He seemed to understand our need for experiences. He made us this way and (as it turns out) we believe what we have *experienced,* not necessarily what we have heard or read. To the disciple Thomas, who has for two thousand years been labeled "doubting Thomas," Jesus said, "Come here, Tom. Touch my hands and side and *experience for yourself* that it is really me." There was no condemnation or reproach, just depth of love, understanding, and a desire to connect through an intimate experience with Himself. He hasn't changed in the last two thousand years. He still desires the intimacy of relationship through experiences with Himself. I will suggest an experiential model shortly. But first, I want to tell you about the Jesus I have come to know. I have known Him most of my life (since age five) as a baptized believer. It has been more recently that I have come to know Him experientially and intimately.

A Funk

I had felt this way for days, but was not allowing myself to actually experience the discomfort. I was in the car, heading somewhere on the freeway, when I finally allowed myself to realize that *I was in a funk.* A funk is when you feel a nagging, emotional discomfort you can't seem to shake or ultimately ignore. We have so many emotional defenses that keep us from feeling this discomfort that, when we actually feel the funk, the defenses aren't working well. When I drive my car, it has a certain relaxing effect (assuming there is minimal traffic, right kids?). I am able to think about things that I haven't had time to think about otherwise. This day I found myself in a funk. Being a counselor and one who teaches others about being *emotionally intelligent*, I summoned my ability of introspection, looking at the events of the past twenty-four to forty-eight hours, hoping to find what had triggered me into this funk. In the past, I have found a repressed anger caused by a grocery cashier being curt or obnoxious. Usually I think of some witty rebuttal and soon feel better. Sometimes it's a story from a counselee that triggers some of my own issues which are yet unresolved. This time, however, I couldn't find any triggers.

For a time, I was resigned to my "funk thinking" of *this too shall pass.* Then it dawned on me that while *I* didn't know why I felt the way I did, my creator (who knows my thoughts from afar, Psalms 139) did know. Why didn't I ask Him? So I did. It was only a few seconds before I found myself in a memory I hadn't thought of in perhaps thirty years. It was Thanksgiving vacation and I was in the seventh grade. My family had made the pilgrimage to the homestead my grandfather had built in Pennsylvania. It was a big, red brick house set on a hill (everything is on a hill in Pa.). I was down below the house on a cinder road, tossing a football with my cousin. In a moment, I knew why the Holy Spirit had taken me *back there*, because I remembered exactly what I had felt that day. It was the *same feeling* I was currently having and the cause of my funk. Just before leaving on break, one of my teachers had assigned a paper that was due when I returned. Being passive-aggressive, I had "forgotten" to bring the information I needed to do the paper. As I threw the football with my cousin, I was dreading my return to class without my paper.

Then I asked the Lord to reveal Himself to me in the memory. When I looked up, I saw Him sitting on the hill just below the house, watching my cousin and me throw the football. I am always happy and surprised to see Jesus in my memories. I know that perhaps many of you don't believe it was actually Jesus whom I saw. But, it was He. For, you see, I am one of His sheep and I both know His voice and recognize His presence. He was wearing a long, bright white robe. He had long, flowing hair and a beard. He was leaning back somewhat, holding one of His knees, relaxing as if he was watching a ball game at a picnic.

I looked up and said, "Jesus, what are you doing here?" He answered that He was watching me throw the football. Being surprised that He would take the time to just watch me throw a football, I asked why. His body posture changed and He leaned toward me with a somewhat serious look on His face. "You need to understand something," He said. "I created you with the ability and desire to throw a football. I am enjoying watching you do what I created you to do." Wow! That thought had absolutely never occurred to me: that Jesus would be *interested enough* to sit and watch me merely toss around a football and that this was *the way He made me.* However, I still had a problem. I looked back at Jesus and decided to share what I was feeling. "Yeah," I said, "but what about the paper?" Shrugging His shoulders, Jesus looked at me and said, "It (the paper) wasn't my idea." Wow again! Jesus, the creator of the universe, was more interested in watching me throw a football than write a paper. I knew then that He was also speaking into my current circumstance. The funk I was experiencing was triggered by doing all the things I *had to do* and seldom having time to do the things I *wanted to do.* Jesus was reminding me that it was important to pursue the interests and talents He had created in me. Furthermore, He was giving me permission to do just that.

Barriers To Relationship Removed

I was reminded again of Jesus' original intent when He created us: relationship and blessing. That relationship was interrupted at the fall. Barriers were built. The effects of our choice to join satan's rebellion were felt in the depths of our souls. We came to believe that God *did not* create us for relationship. But if there *were* a relationship, it was our responsibility to initiate it. Intermediaries were put in positions of authority to tell us what God wanted us to know. If we wanted to be in right relationship with Him, we needed to follow His rules of life and sacrifice. Remember: all of that changed at the cross. Jesus (Himself) came to tell us of the Father's original intent and demonstrated it throughout His earthly ministry. He came to redeem, restore, and heal. He became *our* sacrifice, the curtain was torn from top to bottom, and God removed the barriers Himself.

Then He sent the Holy Spirit to dwell in and among us. We could seek and find Him. However, it was hard to believe that Relational Rule Number One could actually be true. Four thousand years of history had resulted in ingrained, entrenched deceptions by the enemy and the co-opting of the institutions of this world by man and satan.

Barriers Now Imbedded In Our Souls

The barriers still remain, but now they are embedded deep in our own hearts and souls. What happens when the Holy Spirit speaks new truth to us? It is important to give ourselves *permission* to accept and believe. We give notice to our emotions that we will no longer act on what we now know to be lies. When we take inventory of the damage caused by the old, false beliefs, we will be astounded at how much they have cost us. What I am suggesting is that we seek for Him and see if God does not respond. The model is quite simple.

A Connection Model

We don't need a tremendous amount of structure to connect relationally with our creator. God is a Spirit and (just as it was in the garden) it is our spiritual mind and body that connect with Him. The model is intended to assist in that process of connecting you with the Lord. We will be entering the spirit world. There is no need to fear, for God is, of course, the Lord of all creation including the realm of the spirit. Although I will be a guide (of sorts) for you in this process, this will *not* be "new age type," spirit-guided imagery. Instead, it is inviting the Holy Spirit to direct a work of restoration and healing in you. I am inviting you to allow the Lord to come; but the choice, of course, is yours. If this is not the right time for you, I understand. The Holy Spirit and I are both gentlemen, and there will be nothing forced upon you.

Safety & Confidentiality Essential

The essentials here are safety and confidentiality. This is between you and Him. I can guarantee you that He only *knocks* at your heart's door; He never forces His way in. I can guess what you might be thinking: "Didn't I let Jesus into my heart at the moment of salvation?" The answer is yes. I am suggesting, however, that that was the *front* door. The doors I am talking about are the various doors leading to the rooms of your soul, the places where the memories, wounds, and beliefs are stored. We are going to ask Jesus to come into those places. Again I remind you that He only comes by invitation.

Note: This model is a simplified version of many different inner healing models suggested by many wonderful teachers including David Seamens, the McNutts, the Sandfords, Leanne Payne, John Winber, Ed Smith (Theophostic), and Terry Wardel.

Inner Healing

Inner Healing is the healing of memories, both experiential and genetic, that are recorded as events in our minds with emotions and interpretations attached. The painful part of the memory is usually the emotion attached to the interpretation. Emotions are the key, and remember: they know no time. Current emotions are connected to past pain. As I mentioned, the Holy Spirit is a gentleman; He will not override your will. You may be angry with God, afraid of Him, or full of shame and unwilling to let the creator of the universe into those private rooms of your soul. It is all right. Jesus will knock and wait at the door.

If you are ready, then find a safe, quiet place. Usually I ask people to close their eyes. But since I am not there to talk you through this, I suggest that you read through the simple steps first, and then refer to them as you go through the process. If by chance you are reading this book and are not a "believer" this process will work for you, too. Just invite the creator of the universe, Jesus, to come into your heart. Simply confess your need for redemption from sins of both survival and/or rebellion. The blood (don't get hung up here) Jesus shed on the cross covers it all. I am not oversimplifying or minimizing Jesus work on the cross. Simply stated, Jesus sacrifice was God Himself initiating and shaping relationship with us and assuming full responsibility. He's waiting.

First Invite the Holy Spirit

First we invite the Holy Spirit and give Him permission to walk the corridors of our souls, searching out the room containing the memory He wants to bring to our awareness. Sometimes a memory comes to our mind quickly; other times, it starts out as a distant vista on the edge of our awareness. It is okay; just let yourself become aware of the memory. I have found for myself and in conversations with others that these memories often are *surprise* memories of which we haven't thought in many years. This is just God affirming His presence and reaffirming His sovereignty. He knows where the lies are locked away.

Wait & Watch

Frequently we attempt to help the Holy Spirit at this point. There are memories that we know probably affect our souls and need to be healed. Consequently, we desire to go to those memories, thinking that they must be what God wants to heal. Sometimes these are the memories God wants to heal; sometimes they are not. Spend a little time waiting and watching to be sure. When I am leading a group in this process or merely praying with an individual, the *watching and waiting* element can be a bit unnerving. What if the Holy Spirit doesn't "show up" with a memory? Remember that there are many reasons that a memory may not surface. It is the creator of the universe we are asking into those vulnerable places in our souls. If you are still waiting fifteen minutes to a half hour later, it is probably time to end the process for the time being.

Bind the Powers Of Darkness

Usually, at this point, I pray a prayer, binding the powers of darkness away from the person and the memory. All authority is given to us, so that whatever we bind on earth will be bound in heaven. Sometimes I do this before inviting the Holy Spirit. You may do either. The point is to be protected from the powers of darkness. These memories were probably traumatic events causing you emotional (and even physical) pain, leaving you very vulnerable. Remember that satan is drawn to pain and trauma like flies to a cow chip. We don't want him mucking around in this process. The power of the enemy of our souls is the power to deceive; he does not want you to be healed and will attempt to harass you with thoughts like: God doesn't love you; He can't be trusted; you are not good enough; you don't deserve to be healed; if you let God into your memories, He will condemn you; and any other lie he thinks you will believe.

When I am praying for someone, I usually pray with my eyes open. There was a time when I believed that if my eyes were open, it wouldn't *count* as praying. I have found though, that I can communicate with my Father both with my eyes open and closed. The reason I keep my eyes open with others is that often, when God is bringing a memory, the *body* will remember first. You will feel yourself or observe others responding bodily to the memory *before* it is clear in their minds. Remember the schoolteacher who was hit on the head with a snowball?

Ask Jesus To Reveal Himself

Once the Holy Spirit has brought the fullness of the memory, it is time to ask Jesus to reveal Himself in the memory. Sometimes there are two (or more) memories. If so, they are usually connected; God will sort it out so that you understand. Remember my memory of Jesus sitting on the hill in Pennsylvania? Inviting Jesus may be a problem. You may reason: if Jesus was there, why didn't He stop bad things from happening? We talked about this in the chapter on control as it relates to free will. All of God's interventions into the "free will" world in which we live have consequences. Even those individuals who perpetrate the *bad things* have free will. It is difficult to understand why God allows bad people to exercise their free will, but He does. This chapter is all about redemption and restoration and healing. Although bad people do bad things, I believe God can and does redeem, restore and heal the chaos and damage that they have done. In no way am I minimizing the atrocities that malicious people have perpetrated on the innocent. Yet I do believe in the awesome power of the creator to redeem, restore and heal.

Not Alone/Comfort & Truth

With the revelation of Jesus in your memory, you realize that you were not really alone when it happened. Much of the pain of the memory is the feeling of abandonment and vulnerability at the time bad things happened. Sometimes just the comfort of his presence is what we need. Only Jesus can truly bring comfort to traumatic memories. When Jesus is there, you are free to talk to Him. Ask Him to speak the truth to you about your interpretation of the event. Remember: the pain is usually in the *interpretation* of the event. Some examples of lies you may believe are: there is something wrong with me; I will be rejected and abandoned; I am unlovable; I will never be cared for; I must work to be worthy and I must do it perfectly. Ask Jesus to remove the pain and affirm His truth.

Bless & Seal, & Then Testify

After Jesus has done His work of comfort, speaking truth, and healing, it is time to be blessed and sealed. If you are alone, just ask Jesus to bless and seal the work of restoration and healing He has just done. It is also time to give testimony to His work. Find a trusted person (spouse, friend or priest/pastor)—someone to whom you may tell your story. This is an important part of the process. If there are embarrassing details you want to omit, then leave them out; but tell your story. Your story becomes *more real in the telling.* Ask this person for their blessing and sealing of the work of grace in your life.

The Battle Isn't Over

God's healing is the taking of spiritual ground in the soul that has been long held by the enemy. He will attempt to take it back. So let your mind dwell on the truths and promises of God's word: I will never leave or forsake you; I have not given you a spirit of fear; God did not send His Son into the world to condemn you; I have plans to prosper and not harm you. Make Psalms and Proverbs your daily bread.

In this process of allowing the reality of what God did and is doing, ask yourself the question: what has this old belief, rooted in lies, cost me? Usually the answer is that the lies have cost us huge portions of our lives, allowing the locust to devour large chunks of our relationships.

Endings & Beginnings = The Process

Like many things in life, the end is just a beginning. As you and God pursue this relationship together, your life will begin to change.

Now that Jesus has done a work in your soul, it will be the first of many. Inner healing is a process. A story I often share is about a man who broke his arm. Sitting in the emergency room and in some pain, he looked up at the doctor who (after resetting the break) was applying the plaster cast. "Doc," he said, " will I be able to play the violin?" The doctor was kind and reassuring, telling him that when the arm was healed and the cast removed, that his arm would be as good as new, maybe even better. He would have no trouble playing the violin. "That's really good, Doc," the man responded, "because I could never play the violin before."

Inner healing is the *beginning* of a life-long process of restoration, redemption and healing. Many think that once they are healed, everything in their lives will be different and they *will now know how to play the violin.* They assume that they will know how to take control of their emotions and, consequently, their relationships. Furthermore, since their relationship with the Lord is no longer inhibited by sin, they can expect the resolution of their longings, in short, paradise. But, as sports commentator Lee Corso likes to say, "Not so fast, my friend." There is much more to it than that. Our life is like *hanging on a vine while our fruit ripens.* God has much to teach us about the way things are (beginning now and lasting forever). Inner healing *removes the diseased part* and allows the fruit to begin to absorb the nutrients. It needs to grow and mature, however, and withstand the seeming capriciousness of life and nature.

Only God Heals

Inner healing is just like the physical healing that I once heard described by a physician: " I don't heal anyone," reported the doctor. "What I do is to remove the hindrances to health, allowing the restorative powers God created into the body to do the healing."

Without an understanding of the core issues of Authority/ Dependency, how can we relate to this hierarchical world that God has created? Without an understanding of how powerful and deceptive the emotions within us can be (and without permission to actually feel and understand them) how can we ever hope to begin to control them in a healthy way? Without knowing the power of the longings within us, where they come from, or that God Himself created us with an expectation of care, how can we begin to come to any resolution of these longings in our souls? How will we ever feel any sense of control and well being, knowing so little of how to put together the jumbled and confused puzzle of our souls?

We have to go to the original source, the creator of this universe, in order to obtain the answer to *why things are the way they are.* He is actually waiting for us to respond by our own choice (through an act of our will) to Him, the One who initiates and shapes the quality of relationship we long for in the depth of our souls. *This One* has accepted all responsibility for that relationship and removed all that could ever stand in the way.

Acknowledgments

First and foremost I want to acknowledge Valee, my wife and my three children, Annie, Katie and Sonny who allowed me to "practice" on them and attempt to "get it right" as a husband and father.

I would not be writing this were it not for my parents, Bill and Dorothy who gave me life and taught me the faith.

I want to acknowledge my sister-in-law, Ann Cobler, who gave of her time to proof read and provide all the expertise I needed to make my thoughts presentable and readable.

Finally I want to acknowledge Liz for her generosity in providing all the tools and support I needed to make this book happen.